CHRONICLING
STANKONIA

CHRONICLING STANKONIA

THE RISE OF THE HIP-HOP SOUTH

REGINA N. BRADLEY

THE UNIVERSITY OF NORTH CAROLINA PRESS *Chapel Hill*

This book was published with the assistance of the Fred W. Morrison Fund of the University of North Carolina Press.

Set in Chaparral and Chronic by Westchester Publishing Services

The University of North Carolina Press has been a
member of the Green Press Initiative since 2003.

Library of Congress Cataloging-in-Publication Data
Names: Bradley, Regina N., 1984– author.
Title: Chronicling Stankonia : the rise of the hip-hop South /
  Regina N. Bradley.
Description: Chapel Hill : University of North Carolina Press, 2021. |
  Includes bibliographical references and index.
Identifiers: LCCN 2020022370 | ISBN 9781469661957 (cloth : alk. paper) |
  ISBN 9781469661964 (paperback : alk. paper) | ISBN 9781469661971 (ebook)
Subjects: LCSH: Rap (Music)—Social aspects—Southern States. | Rap
  (Music)—Southern States—History and criticism. | Hip-hop—Southern
  States. | African Americans—Race identity—Southern States. | OutKast
  (Musical group)
Classification: LCC ML3918.R37 B715 2021 | DDC 782.4216490975—dc23
LC record available at https://lccn.loc.gov/2020022370

Cover illustration: *Chronicling Stankonia* by Stacey A. Robinson. Used by permission of the artist.

Chapter 3 was previously published in a different form as "Re-Imagining Slavery in the Hip-Hop Imagination," *south: a scholarly journal* 49, no. 1 (Fall 2016): 3–24.

For Eugene and Sara Barnett, who made it cool to be southern

For Roy, the truly OutKasted one

And, as always, for Ayana Siera

In Loving Memory:

Reginald K. Barnett, my Daddy,

   who taught me music and friendship is essential to the soul

Terrell Anthony Warrior, the original playa with game

Marco Mason, who showed me why they don't dance no mo'

Larry "DJ Shock" Sanders, who was truly cooler

   than a polar bear's toenails

Bend corners like I was a curve, I struck a nerve

And now you bout to see this southern playa serve

. . .

—Big Boi, "ATLiens"

CONTENTS

Yoh Phillips, Jah Lee, Maurice Garland, Rodney Carmichael, Panama Jackson, Mike Jordan, and Ed Garnes. A very special thank you to DJ Jelly, DJ Jaycee, Dee Dee Hibbler, and D. L. Warfield for their encouragement to complete this book.

I also want to thank my kinfolks across the souf 'cause we the proof the South got something to say: the first ladies of Alabama, Qiana Cutts, Quinita Morrow, and Imani Perry; them Alabama boys, Derrais Carter and Maurice Hobson; the crooked letta squad outta Mississippi, Kiese Laymon, Jesmyn Ward, Jarvis McInnis, Julius Fleming, Charlie Braxton, John Jennings, Kirsten West Savali, Brad Franklin, David Dennis, and B. Brian Foster; my Louisiana people, Brittney Cooper, Yaba Blay, Shantrelle Lewis, Randall Jelks, Courtney Bryan, and Kinitra Brooks; the first ladies of Texas, Josie Pickens, Karen Good Marable, Ashanté Reese, Melanye Price, Melynda Price, LaVeda Thomas; them Texas boys, Maco Faniel, Robert Hodge, my little bro Stevie Johnson, TaShawn Thomas, and Langston Colin Wilkins; FLAWDA cousins, Fredara Hadley, Susana Morris, Elliott Powell, Ducarmel Saint Louis, Jenny Saint Louis, Nicole Symmonds, and Will McKinney; Dasan Ahanu, David Ikard, Matthew Morrison, Scott Heath, and my girls Robin Boylorn, L. H. Stallings, and Candice Benbow, holding down North Cackalacky; I see you cousins Wade F. Dean, Naima Cochrane, Nashia Whittenburg, and Ahmad Washington over there with South Cackalacky on your backs; Quentin Blanton Sr. holding down Ar-kan-sas; Asha Boo French and Chesya Burke, who represent Kentucky, thank you for your thoughtfulness in my dark moments; this generation's Zora aka Zandria Robinson (Swear), Tauheed Rahim II, Jamey Hatley, K. T. Ewing, Earle Fisher, and Gee Joyner, the thought leaders of the Ten-a-key/Tennessee mafia. Shout-out to my Virginia people 'nem J. T. Roane, Aisha Durham, C. J. Woody, Chelsey Culley-Love, Holly Smith, and Tammy Kernodle.

I am overwhelmed by the academic love and support I have received over the duration of this project. Thank you to *Sounding Out!* and *Black Perspectives* for the opportunity to write about OutKast in the early stages of this book and *south* journal for the first printing of "Re-Imagining Slavery in the Hip-Hop Imagination." Thank you to Mark Simpson-Vos, editor extraordinaire, and the good folks at the University of North Carolina Press for their constant encouragement. Mark first heard about this book during the 2014 MLA annual meeting where I was desperately on the job market and trying to come up with a book idea. He graciously met with me and my uneven ideas and

ACKNOWLEDGMENTS

Acknowledgments are always the hardest thing for me to write because I'm southern, community is everything, and I wanna thank er'body who has ever gave me a smile, a nod, a hug, or small word of support! I'ma try though. I want to thank Albany, GA, the 'Bany, the city fighting to prove why it's still got good life and lives, for their support and love throughout my entire life. Shout-out to my 'Bany family: Doris Cross, Henretta Benson, Aileen Harris, Stephanie Harris-Jolly, Woody and Jeanette Givens, Susie Beach, Gloria Anderson, Charity Anderson, Suzy Seay, GQ Wallace, Shirley Vaughn, my Hines Memorial Christian Methodist Episcopal Church family, Farris and Obzeine Shorter, Dee Luke, Warren Luke Sr., my Albany State University family (I love you Stephanie Hankerson! Ram Fam we RUN THIS SHOW!!), Velsenna King, Andrea Towns, Curnesia Bogans, my cuzzo Elizabeth Mitchell, the dean Ontario Wooden, and them Dunlap guhs Cheremie, Chelcie, Chenae, and Charlene and Patricia Dunlap. I love you Leslie Givens, Charles King Jr., Angelica Fowler-King, Tara Bell, Corbin King, Archie Fowler, Melanie Shorter-Jones, Kanese Rachel, Rashaunda Flemming, Dwan Ashe, Kameelah Martin, Greg Mitchell, Arkesia Jenkins, Booker Jones, Toussaint Hill, Ron Simmons, Andrea Avery, André Mitchell, Bradford Gamble, Jasmyne Walker, Erin Menefee, Arrica King, Ashley Scott, Yoshi Dunn, and Arin Harper. A heartfelt "Aaaaaaaaaye" to my Georgia OTP (Outside the Perimeter) squad 'cause we outchea!: them Valdosta boys Trent James and Selwyn James; Geniquiya Meredith, Sandra Meredith, Melody Keeton, Sarah Hall, Rosa and Larry Burrus, Erika Estrada, Jabari Ben, Robert "Blue" Williams, Chris Jones, Nikk Nelson, Cullen Carson, Foster Carson, Albert Whitehead, Seymore Harrison, Charles Davis, and Randy Williams. I wouldn't be here without my personal Dungeon Family, my ATL kinfolk Birgitta Johnson, Brandon Manning, Leroy Thompson IV, Justin Hosbey, Sam Arnold, Charlotte Arnold, Derek Arnold, Gabrielle Fulton-Ponder, Danielle Deadwyler, Charlotte Conner, Robert Miller, Aurielle Lucier, Terence Turner, Joan Collier, Kym Wallace, Carl Manson, the Bottom of the Map podcast squad "Super Producer" Floyd Hall, Stephen "Major" Key, Christina "Young Savage" Lee, Je-Anne Berry, Ayanna "Shortcake" Taylor, Christine Dempsey, John Haas, Fahamu Pecou, Charles Nichols, Craig Bogle, the late Fred McElroy (continue to rest well), and Audrey and John McCluskey.

Shout-out to my good people 'nem Scott Poulson Bryant, Darnell Moore, Zaheer Ali, Eric Darnell Pritchard, Carl Suddler, Pableaux Johnson, Seneca Vaught, Rudy Aguilar, Donald Coleman, Myke Johns, Lois "O.G." Reitzes, Yen Rodriguez, Charles Hughes, Joe Schloss, Tamara Palmer, Matt Davis, Kimmie Bowers, Curtis Byrd, Alexis Pauline Gumbs, Sam Livingston, Akiba Solomon, Roger Sneed, Carla Shedd, LeConte Dill, Tef Poe, La Marr Bruce, Charles McKinney, Utz McKnight, Kaye Whitehead, Tiffany Lethabo King, LaKeyta Bonnette-Bailey, Ernest L. Gibson III, Clint Fluker, Adam Banks, Reynaldo Anderson, Erich Nunn, Shanté Smalls, Andy Crank, Pete Kunze, David Davis, Chanda Prescod-Weinstein, Kendra Mitchell, and Martha Diaz.

Special shout-out to my sister squad who holds me down when I can't see myself: my besties of twenty-plus years Erica Bridley, Courtney Holman, Amber Hayes, Mama Sylvia Wright, Nina Warrior, Vernita Beach, Kyra Lassiter, Roleta Lassiter, Patina Bridley, Jervai Dumas, Treva Lindsey, Bettina Love, Bianca Keaton, Natina Hill, Alisha Lola Jones, Aja Burrell Wood, Nashara Mitchell, Tanisha Ford, Gholdy Muhammad, Siobhan Carter-David, Heidi Renee Lewis, Joan Morgan, Jessica Marie Johnson, Courtney Baker, Tiffany Pogue, Kaila Story, Michelle Hite, Stephanie Evans, Andrea Jackson Gavin, Amrita Chakrabarti-Myers, Jo Davis-McElligat, Aletha Carter, Tamura Lomax, Timothy Anne Burnside, Camika Royal, Portia Hemphill, LaKisha Simmons, Aisha Durham, Gaye Theresa Johnson, Rashida Govan, Asia Leeds, Monica White, Emily Lordi, Jenny Stoever, Nat Duncan, Rosie Uyola, Liana Silva, JoyEllen Williams, Lynn Washington, Sheila Smith McKoy, Griselda Thomas, Corrie Davis, Nichole Guillory, Roxanne Donovan, Ashley Gilmore, Mia Charlene White, Julia Mallory, Tawana Jennings, Crown Williams, Sarah Jackson, Courtney Marshall, Nafissa Thompson-Spires, Tasha Harrison, Rakia Marcus, Shanell Luke, Erika Lawrence, Ariel Johnson, and the "Maes" Toni Arnold, Brittany Manson, Gabrielle Jones, Sheena Burrus, and Chiquita Safford. A very special thank you and "namaste" to Octavia Raheem and Andreka Peat. Shine bright, sistren. I love y'all!

Finally, I had to build myself up to thank my blood and chosen family. I call out the names of my Paw Paw, Daddy, and Daddy-in-Law Roy Bradley Sr. Please take this book as a living testimony to the love and magic you pumped into me my life. May you continue to rest well. Asé. To my Nana Boo, Sara Barnett, I often fret about how to show you a sliver of the immense gratitude that I have for you. May this book be boom! Here we are. Thank you so much Mark. I also want to extend a special thanks to Joseph Parsons for helping me through the proposal and initial revision process. Your kind words and suggestions are more than appreciated.

I am indebted to the Harvard University Hutchins Center for African American Research, especially the Harvard Hiphop archive. Thank you so much to Skip Gates and his fire ass Tesla, Abby Wolfe, Krishna Lewis, Harold Shawn, and the wondrous Marcyliena Morgan for their support and encouragement of this book. Thank you all around to my colleagues in the department of English at Kennesaw State University. I also want to give a special thanks to my OutKast class students for helping me massage my ideas into solid analysis. Special thank yous to my former students Jeff Wallace, Sheldon McCarthy, Jaron Whitehead, Tyler Moore, Eugene Crump, Jaylen Hiller, Donovan McKelvey, Sean Shields, Autumn Patterson, Dasia Jones, Selina Keith, Himie Freeman, Meshach Young, and Vaughn Robinson for our music and life discussions. A very special thank you to my research assistants Aquila Campbell and Kelsey Provow for their assistance during the completion of this project.

I want to thank the scholars and critics who enthusiastically listened to me work through my ideas and offered words of sustenance and/or read various drafts of this book at its different stages: Mark Anthony Neal (MAAAAAN!), Guthrie Ramsey (I luh you Dr. Guy!), Kellie Jones, Sharon Holland, Sharon Harley, Stacey Robinson, Nicole Fleetwood, Shana Redmond, Maureen Mahon, Anthony Pinn, Barry Shank, Jeffrey McCune, Karida Brown, Todne Thomas, Greg Tate, Ken Wissoker, Blair Kelley, Talitha LeFlouria, Therí Pickens, Candice Jenkins, Joycelyn Moody, Sonja Laneheart, Daphne Brooks, Keeanga Yamahtta Taylor, C. Riley Snorton, Dwan Reese, Chris Emdin, Karl Hagstrom Miller, Kimberly Wallace-Sanders, Karen Marie Mason, Ruth Nicole Brown, Jack Hamilton, Matt Sakakeeny, Emery Petchauer, Daniel HoSang, Loren Kajikawa, Ruth Wilson Gilmore, Andre Carrington, Eric Weisbard, Ann Powers, Jeffrey "O.G. O.G. Triple O.G." Ogbar, Andre Brock, the good doctor brothers Howard Rambsy and Kenton Rambsy, Elaine "Docta E" Richardson, Cynthia Dillard, Erica Armstrong Dunbar, Dumi Lewis, Marc Lamont Hill, Jim Smethurst, Ali Colleen Neff, Justin Burton, Margo Natalie Crawford, Kai Green, Walter Kimbrough, Lester Spence, Noliwe Rooks, Lisa B. Thompson, Gwendolyn Pough, Robert Jones Jr., Tamika L. Carey, Eve Dunbar, David Leonard, Lisa Guerrero, Karen L. Cox, Julius Bailey, Ashon Crawley, Oliver Wang, Sarita Gregory, Valerie Grim, Portia Maultsby, a physical representation of the eternal love I always have for you in my heart and soul. Thank you so much, Nana Boo my love! Shout-out to my number-one fans: my mommy, Ilona Sullivan, Reggie Sullivan, Roscoe Washington, and Teolar Bradley. Thank you to the fierce ones who are my auntie squad: Deidre Ingram, Dorothy Woody, Ernestine Lassiter, Candy Hayes, Barbara Rodolph, and Linda Stephenson. Shout-out to my uncles Werner, Larry, Norbert, Don, Rick Stephenson, Everett Hayes, and Craig Woody. I love you sissy aka Ebony Washington! Also sending a love note to my brothers Isaiah Washington and Jeremy Ingram. I'd also like to extend a warm thank you to my chosen brothers Warren Luke, Clifford Marcus, John L. Williams, Rickie Frazier, Brian Dawson Sr., Quinton S. Beach Sr., Ellis Dumas III, Cameron Beatty, Jeremy Gilmore, Joseph French, Vincent Mosley, Keith Mosley, and Jonathon Lawrence. So much love to my mini-village, my nephews and nieces, who make my life bright. I love you! I'm one of those dog people: thank you to my fur babies and best writing partners ever Winnie and Lovie and my two babies who crossed the rainbow bridge Roxy and Lady Bug. To my daughter Ayana, thank you for being my biggest motivator. Go out into the world and be dope, Diva Daughter! I am so thankful we chose each other. I love you.

I saved the best for last. Roy Bradley, my king, my world, my every-thing, your name might as well be on the cover of this book too. I love you, babe. Ain't no Dr. Regina Bradley without Roy Bradley, bih! Thank you, thank you, THANK Y'ALL! If I've forgotten anyone, charge it to my head not my heart.

INTRODUCTION
THE MOUNTAINTOP AIN'T FLAT

I first fell in love with OutKast at the age of fourteen in the summer of 1998, right before my freshman year of high school. I had recently moved to live with my grandparents and father in Albany, Georgia, a small city in the southwest corner of the state. Albany was much slower-paced than my previous residence in northern Virginia, but I wasn't completely unfamiliar with it. I knew that my name was not Regina but "Mr. (or Mrs.) Barnett's granddaughter," that attending my church, Hines Memorial CME (Christian Methodist Episcopal), on Sunday meant staying for Sunday school and regular service, and that Albany's heat was wet, held on tight like my favorite aunties, and didn't understand personal boundaries. I transferred to Southside Middle School in the spring, and people did not let me forget that. I had the allure of the "new girl" working in my favor, but I was treading water trying to find somewhere to fit in when everyone was already situated and looking forward to high school. Further, I was a bit apprehensive about letting my guard down: I was mercilessly bullied at my former school and suffered terribly low self-esteem, while working through heavy anxiety and the guilt of leaving my younger brother and sister behind with their dad in Virginia. My schoolmates laughed at my accent and fast enunciation and laughed harder when I tried to dance, equally jerky and quick with my body at the end-of-year dance. Girls chuckled and dudes raised their eyebrows in amusement while dancing behind the popular girls who "danced right." A girlfriend pulled me aside and told me matter-of-factly, "Chile, you wound up. You talk too fast! You dance too fast! You listen too fast! You just too wound up." I learned quickly how to slow it down: "Shorty" was "Shawty." "Girl" was "guh." "Back" was "bike." And, in addition to being my folks' granddaughter, I was described as "that tall, smart, high yellow guh" and later, "Gina Mae." Gina Mae happened by accident, starting as a joke meant to tone down my northeasternness and officially dub me a southern girl. "We gone get you right, Gina Mae," my new classmates said, often with a wink and a drawn-out laugh. Their intention wasn't mean or ill-spirited, which I had accepted as the norm in my previous middle school. I grew to love my nickname and eventually let my guard down.

Upon letting my guard down I quickly realized that I was transitioning into the South through two sets of experiences: my own southernness and that of my grandparents, which was centered on growing up in the Jim Crow South. My grandmother Sara and my grandfather Eugene were among the first black educators to integrate the Dougherty County School System. My grandmother's ministry was to be ladylike, and her sharp eye for detail about how I presented myself was no doubt rooted not only in her own affinity for beauty but also in retaliation that might arise if black children didn't reflect a "proper" upbringing. My grandfather was more about the business of being successful—education was the heralded portal to success for my young black self. He warned me about falling short of my potential and how I was "too smart and too pretty" not to do well in school. "Your job is them books," he scolded with a smile. My grandparents translated their understandings of southernness into their own unique love languages that were grounded in their upbringing in northeast Georgia and southwest Georgia, respectively. Their weariness of white folks, strong advocacy of education and academic excellence, and hyperfocus on developing and sustaining my respectability framed my daily interactions with my friends and classmates. However, a point of departure from my folks' influence on how I viewed the South was hip-hop.

In the mornings before school started, we were corralled into the school gym. A country fried cacophony of laughter, yelling, cursing, and freestyling pulled me in. My squad and I sat in the top right section of the bleachers where the people-watching was best. Some of the kids stomped their feet as they rapped or argued about lyrics to a song by OutKast, Goodie Mob, or somebody on the seemingly infinite list of artists on No Limit Records. Other students rapped their own bars, quickly moving their arms, pointing at themselves and whomever they were battling, and smacking their hands on their chests. On the gym floor, folks played basketball if the gym monitors were feeling particularly gracious while the less-than-spectacular hoopsters stayed on the sidelines and gave commentary on the game.

It was equally loud after school because Monroe Comprehensive High School was next door and the sound of subwoofers thrumming in old-school Chevy Caprices, beat-up pickups, and crappy Toyotas rolling quickly over cracked cement speed bumps in the school parking lot crashed through the verbal warnings and stares of teachers not to venture over to the "high school side." I made mental notes of the rapper folks continuously in my ear: OutKast, Three 6 Mafia, UGK, Goodie Mob, and bass artists like DJ Smurf, DJ Kizzy Rock, and Uncle Luke.

Radio mixtapes were still an art and a currency in 1998. I meticulously listened to the radio, careful to avoid recording commercials and to leave just enough quiet space to move from track to track. Among my favorite tracks was Goodie Mob's "Black Ice." Besides the bass kick, high electric-guitar notes, and organ reminding me of a gospel song, the swishing sound reminded me of the cicadas that sung from the treetops outside of my folks' house. We lived in the country, outside of Albany's city limits. The cicadas would sing loud enough that at moments they harmonized with the swishing on the "Black Ice" track. Additionally, "Black Ice" was the first time I took a hard listen to OutKast: the swagger of Antwan "Big Boi" Patton and André "3000" Benjamin's effortless yet layered cadence jumped from the track. I fell in love with their voices because they melted and eased into my ear like the voices of my classmates.

However, it wasn't until marching-band camp at my school Westover High that I truly became "OutKasted." While marching band didn't pan out—I ended up being a solid equipment manager for the season—my interaction with Rodney, a senior and one of the trumpet section leaders, jumpstarted my love for OutKast. During a lunch break, I found Rodney cross-legged and silently tapping his fingers against his leg and trumpet. He nodded spontaneously and scribbled on a sprawl of papers in front of him. When I got closer, I heard a soft hum that he emphasized at the end by poking the pencil in the air in front of him:

Ba da bump bump buh!
Ba da bump bump buh!
Ba da bump bump bump bum buh!

"Hi, Rodney!" I squealed with a bit too much enthusiasm. He didn't raise his head from what he was doing.

"Oh. Hi."

"What you doing?"

"Transcribing this song for the stands." Stand music was the popular music played by the band and heard on the radio between plays and after the band's formal show at football games. Rodney goes back to humming.

"What song is that?"

"SpottieOttieDopalicious."

I muster up enough courage to ask him one more question. "Who's it by?"

Rodney looked up with an annoyed expression on his face. I couldn't tell if it was because I was bothering him while he was transcribing or because I was a freshman.

"OutKast."

"That's tight!" I squeaked. Rodney didn't respond. The silence was my cue to get gone.

I would have other daily encounters with OutKast in high school, such as through my friend Brandon, a then aspiring emcee, who would blend and riff his own rhymes with OutKast's music. For example, while the rest of the class found Brandon's sudden use of André's ending bars from Cool Breeze's song "Watch for the Hook" an amusing start to the beginning of the final Spanish exam, our teacher did not, and chided us in English *and* Spanish. OutKast, along with an army of southern artists behind them, introduced me to the post–civil rights era South. And, above all else, that contemporary southern culturescape was distinctively and intentionally grounded in hip-hop.

When the Mountaintop Ain't Flat: Recognizing a Hip-Hop South

Hip-hop was my means of personal and cultural transition into being southern. Not until a decade later would I find the language to articulate—or recognize—that my fondness of southern hip-hop and OutKast was a segue into the larger question of where the South fit into not only hip-hop culture but contemporary American society in general. The black American South seldom has room to expand past three major historical touchstones: the antebellum era, Jim Crow, and the modern civil rights movement. Non-southerners take comfort and pleasure in being able to restrict black identities to these markers of southernness because of their accessible narratives, romanticization in mainstream American culture, and lagging agency outside of a white imagination. In the same way that the American South embraces being a regional poltergeist, living with and benefiting from the haunts of the past, southern black folks too are haunted by white people. Southern blacks are expected to cower in the shadows of racism, succumb to their believed innate backwardness, and live in daily terror simply for being black in the South. They are seldom viewed as their own complex and autonomous selves. Without question, black folks are believed to "fall in" with southern whites' experiences. This extends from the antebellum era into modern times, as southern blacks continuously fight to carve room for themselves to speak their truth to power. Even amid the struggles of the twentieth-century civil rights movement, itself an effort to depart from white supremacy and the sociocultural constructs that supported it, white folks and their reactions were not far from center. The legibility of southern black respectability politics aside, the movement sustained itself across the region both because of the promise of black civil rights and the hope of white folks' assimilation into the effort that these rights would be better for everyone.

However, after the assassination of Dr. Martin Luther King Jr. and the collapse of a perceived monolithic black leadership, the coordinated efforts of the movement broke down into localized attempts that, by themselves, did not sustain the interest of national news media (black or white). This was especially true in Albany, the peculiar jewel of the civil rights movement that forced Dr. King to reconsider his blueprint for racial equality.[1] Although my grandparents did not participate on the front lines of the movement, they knew people who did, and they contributed to the cause through other means such as making protest posters, donating money, or providing brown-bag lunches. Further, it was not uncommon that teachers and elders who participated in the movement were still living in Albany, such as Rutha Mae Harris, who taught special education at Monroe Comprehensive High School, or the late Dr. Janie Rambeau, who taught French at Westover High. Landmarks were also important during the Albany movement: for example, the Albany Civil Rights Museum on Whitney Avenue was repurposed from its use as a church headquarters to be used for marchers and protestors. Without fail, every time we drove past the museum my grandparents would point to it and the Shiloh Baptist Church across the street and say, "When Dr. King was here, he would walk back and forth across the street to speak to both churches because all the people couldn't fit into just one building." Although I would nod and say "yes ma'am" or "yes sir" out of respect, it was fleeting in my mind because I did not feel an attachment to the movement with the same fervor and depth that my grandparents and elders did. However, what went unsaid was very much a part of my daily experiences: Albany's high unemployment rate, the threat and fear of becoming a teenage mother or high school dropout, racial profiling, and the rap music that spoke to these socioeconomic conditions daily. In my mind, Reverend Dr. Martin Luther

King Jr. held space alongside the Atlanta rapper Pastor Troy, who proclaimed, "Ain't no mo play in G-A," and dubbed himself "leader of the wicked church."[2] While Troy's imagery certainly subverts the southern tradition of the black church as the epicenter of protest and change and its associated respectability politics, there is also an awareness that he too is speaking his truth to power, albeit with more bass kicks and synthesizers than a church organ or the traditional percussive clapping of marchers or a church congregation. What southern hip-hop realized and older generations wanted to tone down was that Dr. King's mountaintop was not flat.[3]

Chronicling Stankonia interrogates the cultural expressions of the post–civil rights hip-hop generations, black southerners who are twice removed from the civil rights movement of the 1950s and 1960s and its immediate aftermath in the early 1970s. Specifically, I'm interested in excavating the experiences of black southerners who came of age in the 1980s and 1990s and use hip-hop culture to buffer themselves from the historical narrative and expectations of civil rights movement era blacks and their predecessors. I theorize this sociocultural landscape as the hip-hop South, a hodgepodge of past, present, and future narrations of southern blackness. The hip-hop South combines cornerstones of the past using hip-hop to carve out a space where the complexity of experiences in the post–civil rights era can breathe. The contemporary black South remains uncharted terrain. Southern hip-hop deromanticizes the mountaintop as prime real estate and works it for what it is—an entanglement of race, place, and privileged memories that attempts to thwart the ideas and reflections outside of a "suitable" southern spectrum that remains closely tied to the sociohistorical boundaries of a southern imagination. The hip-hop South carves out room to work through the challenges of existing in the most recent cycles of the post–civil rights South.

Further, it is important to recognize that the bulk of scholarship on post–civil rights black culture focuses on locales outside of the South. For example, Nelson George's introduction of the term "post-soul" in his book *Post-Soul Nation* and Mark Anthony Neal's continuation of that theorization in his study *Soul Babies* primarily examines post-soul and post–civil rights popular culture aesthetics geographically located outside of the South.[4] Zandria Robinson's sociological study of Memphis in her work *This Ain't Chicago* repositions the ideology of post-soul back to the South to mean "post-Soul Blues." Robinson argues that black music is the foundation to realizing and understanding the contemporary southern black experience, situating music as part of a "bodily lexicon of black southern life in the post–civil rights era . . . a set of performa-tive narratives utilized to navigate the contemporary contradictions of the South and racial progress."[5] Returning to the mountaintop meta-phor, for those marching and fighting for access to sociopolitical and economic equality, accessing the mountaintop is a hard-fought win. It is deemed enough for black southerners to have the mountaintop in sight. Once accessed, blacks should have limitless opportunities and few obstacles to the American Dream. Yet post–civil rights black southerners use hip-hop to embrace the fact that the post–civil rights South is complicated and not unproblematic. It is demarcated by the complexity of living interstitially between memories of the past and present. Hip-hop brings into focus the reality that the movement does not smooth out all the bumps in the road or provide a blueprint for navigating more recent obstacles and challenges. The cyclical nature of southern memories—that is, functioning plantations, Civil War re-enactments, and living history museums—is the foundation, but not the totality, of a contemporary southern experience. Thus, hip-hop serves as a powerful intervener to address the continuously shifting ne-gotiations of power, identities, and communities of black people in the South.

Letting the Stank Out: OutKast and the
Rise of the Hip-Hop South

While I do not suggest that hip-hop's presence in the South is the sole marker of its contemporary existence, I do suggest that hip-hop is integral to updating the framework for reading the South's mo-dernity. Although southern hip-hop existed before OutKast, they are the founding theoreticians of the hip-hop South. Their lyrical whimsi-cality and sonic and cultural experimentation with their southernness situates them as the epicenter of recognizing a collective—though not monolithic—contemporary southern black cultural landscape. Fur-ther, OutKast's moniker embraces their (initial) displacement in hip-hop and is an acronym for "Operating under the Krooked American System Too Long."[6] Their embodiment as outcasts can be read on multiple levels, including outcasts of hip-hop's dominant northeastern aesthetics and outcasts as less-than-respectable young black men in the post–civil rights South. Yet OutKast still uses rapping as a tool signifying their existence as young black men, gauging hip-hop as a lens for contemporary scripts of blackness in the present while referring both to the past and the future to annotate their southernness. OutKast's intentional disjuncture of their southernness from the space and time vacuums that often dictate

...na-
...ons
...neta-
...ood shifts paradigms of modernity and urban-
...n-the-fringe narratives of southern blacks. OutKast
...n the use of the South as a renewable source of cultural currency and agency for blacks.

Still, it was not lost on them or their Atlanta-reared and -based producers Organized Noize, consisting of Rico Wade, Patrick "Sleepy" Brown, and Ray Murray, that they needed to demonstrate their awareness of hip-hop's identity as an urban cultural expression that could be used to reflect their experiences in Atlanta. It is important to note that before Organized Noize's efforts to solidify Atlanta's place in hip-hop, the city was already holding its own as a funk music capital: with the help of Bunnie Jackson Ransom, the former wife of Atlanta's first black mayor Maynard Jackson, Atlanta was home to funk music stars like S.O.S. Band, Cameo, and Brick, many of whom migrated to Atlanta to become part of its exploding musical scene.[7] Atlanta's brand of funk intentionally teetered on the line between the sacred and secular, unafraid to blend the aesthetics of faith, trauma, and perseverance in vocal and instrumental performances. This is central to understanding Organized Noize's brand of hip-hop production: Jimmy Brown, the father of group member Sleepy Brown, was an instrumentalist and lead singer for Brick and frequently took a young Sleepy Brown to gigs where he watched from backstage as his father and Brick performed.

As Atlanta grew more visible, so did its arts and culture scenes. While Atlanta was well aware of the hip-hop coming out New York in the 1980s, it wasn't until the arrival of artists like the New York transplant MC Shy D or homegrown talent like Kilo Ali and Raheem the Dream that Atlanta started getting serious about hip-hop.[8]

Even the crossover success of hip-hop acts of groups like Arrested Development and Kris Kross in the early 1990s did not use Atlanta as central to their identity. Arrested Development offered a Bohemian even utopian black southern narrative, pulling from the folk tradition that buoyed southern black cultural expression inside and outside of the South. For example, their hit song "Tennessee" offered a view of country or rural blackness as an escape—for example, playing horseshoes and sitting on the porch—from many of the struggles black folks continued to face in light of the efforts of the movement. Kris Kross relied heavily on their youthful swagger, rooted in their time cruising southwest Atlanta's Greenbriar Mall, where they were discovered by the Atlanta producer and artist Jermaine Dupri. Although rooted in a southern experience, Kris Kross's handlers like Dupri were careful not to make them an act that would have only regional appeal.[9] Intriguingly, however,

Kris Kross's signature aesthetic, wearing their clothes backward and thus suggesting an alternative performance of black boyhood and masculinity, subverts the long-held belief of black southerners as backward and makes it cool. Still, Atlanta remained in pursuit of a solidified hip-hop identity that featured their city's aesthetics and experiences more directly.

Therefore, Atlanta hip-hop artists had a multilayered challenge: Where did hip-hop fit in a largely established narrative of Atlanta as a city of promise and progress for black people? How could hip-hop culture be used to move the South away from the largely held and commercialized legacy of Dr. King? More specifically, producers like Organized Noize and performers like OutKast were inadvertently tasked with the validation of what Imani Perry argues is a contemporary urban South, the creation of a "unique meeting ground of the traditional, the old and new, plus the 'same old, same old.'"[10]

Consider their first album *Southernplayalisticadillacmuzik*. Both Organized Noize and OutKast paid meticulous attention to amplifying—representing—specific locales within the city by sonically and lyrically highlighting Atlanta as southern, urban, and an incubator for hip-hop. For example, on the interlude "Welcome to Atlanta," the fourth track and a skit on album, is a brief musical accompaniment from the previous track "Ain't No Thang," as the captain speaks over a staticky intercom against the sound of the wind outside an airplane. The captain gives an impromptu tour of the city, pointing out not only the blackest and poorest neighborhoods in Atlanta at the time but also significant landmarks that symbolize Atlanta lore. Aside from Atlanta's sports franchises, the captain points out other prevalent business ventures such as the city's position as the "Motown of the South," and as the home of LaFace Records.[11] He also points out the golden dome of Atlanta's capitol and makes sure to acknowledge that it still flies the Confederate battle flag. The captain also points out Decatur, East Point, and College Park, Georgia, the latter two cities running closest to the Atlanta airport and being the homes of Organized Noize and OutKast. In addition, the captain emphasizes the Red Dogs, a drug prevention enforcement program prevalent in the 1980s and 1990s, Cadillacs, and "the playas," an allusion to the next track of the album *Southernplayalisticadillacmuzik* and a signifier of contemporary southern black masculinity.[12] The "Welcome to Atlanta" skit sonically emphasizes Atlanta's urbanity by taking place on what can be read as a commercial airplane flight. It precedes and foreshadows Atlanta's status as the busiest airport in the world. Next, the focal points of the captain's tour blend past and present monikers of southern blackness. The reference to the Confederate flag is significant because it not only reckons with the historical significance of the Confederacy but also hints at the distinction between white and black Southern memories surrounding the flag. The skit's intentional "dirtying" of the South via pairing references to the controversial Red Dog police program's bullying of working-class black communities alongside recognizable white Southern iconography like the Confederate flag grounds Atlanta in contemporaneity as well as in a recognition of the lingering effects of the racial trauma still inflicted on black people in the South.[13] Additionally, the shouting out of multiple communities and subcities that collectively make up Atlanta speaks to its southern urbanity because it references a sprawling urban landscape but also the potential for multiple small communities with urban aesthetics to create a larger urban collective identity.[14]

Still, the lingering effects of the movement and slavery on southern black identities are not lost on OutKast. The track "Myintrotoletuknow" acknowledges the boundaries of past and present in articulating their identities as young southern black men. The diction and phonetic running together of the title allude to the overlap of the past and the present and, at the same time, also mark the way many southerners speak. The track opens with the strike of a gong, signifying both a call to order at the beginning of the album and the importance of what is about to be lyrically delivered. The sound of the gong softens but its urgency still complements an increasingly prominent scratching record and electric and bass guitars. The scratching record signifies OutKast's awareness of hip-hop culture and its touchstones, including deejaying as one of its foundational elements. Yet their lyrics and delivery point to hip-hop as a way of rupturing ideas of black southerners in the past and present. Big Boi rhymes, "Time and time again see I be thinking about that future / Back in the days when we was slaves I bet we was some cool ass niggas."[15] Big Boi's verse acknowledges the continued dominance of slavery as a reference point for understanding southernness but, by postulating that slaves were "some cool ass niggas," he pushes back against defining slavery as solely traumatic. Cool in this sense can be read to mean resilient. Big Boi doubly uses hip-hop as a tool of remembrance: he rhymes about slavery while contextualizing his (and his slave ancestors') cool within hip-hop aesthetics to ease the anxiety associated with slavery. However, he never loses site of *remembering* his ancestors and the trauma associated with slavery. Big Boi repurposes it to parallel his own anxieties about being southern and black in the present. His affirmation of slaves' cool factor is particularly daring as it presents the possibility of slaves' lagging humanity being excavated from their uncovered coolness (an excavation site revisited in recent films like *Django Unchained*, which is discussed in chapter 3 of this book).

André's opening lines respond to and update Big Boi's remembering of the past: "Time is slipping, slowly but surely / Niggas I used to hang with wants to act like they don't know me / Come and listen to my story, I gots a lot of shit up on my mind / I wipe the boo boo from my brain then I finish up my rhyme."[16] André's challenge to "come and listen to my story" parallels Big Boi's remembrance of slavery because he dares the listener to experience his (othered) perspective that does not adhere to a standardized East or West Coast sensibility that grounds hip-hop's identity. Both Big Boi and André buck the status quo, signifying the lack of familiarity with past and current southern sensibilities.

"Myintrotoletuknow" signifies the understanding that there is little cultural or historical distance between the agency of the civil rights movement and the anxieties facing the first wave of post–civil rights generation southern blacks. The U.S. South remains marked by Jim Crow and the antebellum South via the performance of white public history and performance such as plantation tours or reenactments of the Civil War. The historical significance of plantations as genesis points for southern black identities (if not people of color in general) does not bend to the fact that these spaces continue to occupy modern narratives of living and commerce. The ambiguity of tourism and historical signifying alludes to how southernness can only exist in circular spaces that acknowledge and are suited to acknowledging the overlaps of past and present.[17] Slavery is not simply a memory. It is a constantly working cornerstone of purposing black agency and change in southern and even diasporic spaces. The political work of slavery's manifestation in OutKast's rhymes makes hip-hop a tool for connecting contemporary southern blackness to the continued impact of a (global) slave narrative. "Myintrotoletuknow" positions grief not only as a gateway to larger conversations taking place about slavery's continued influence on black identity but also as a way to reconnect past and present manifestations of black agency as a socioeconomic act.

In addition, tracks like "Git Up, Git Out" highlight the challenges of not having access to, or failing to fulfill, the idealistic expectations boasted about in the popular mainstream post–civil rights movement rhetoric of "having overcome." The intentional southern phonetic spelling of "get" as "git" highlights not only hip-hop's re-rendering of language with phonetics but also the (rural) southern expression of "git" as a statement of urgent departure or dismissal. The track opens with Cee-Lo Green singing the chorus, an effort to encourage listeners, under the guise of Cee-Lo talking to his homeboy, to continue moving through the world for their betterment even if they fail in the process. Cee-Lo's verse opens the track, rapping, "I don't recall, ever graduating at all / Sometimes I feel I'm just a disappointment to y'all."[18] I am struck by the double meaning of audience in Cee-Lo's "y'all": it not only signifies the listener but can also denote Cee-Lo's elders or the older generations who heralded education as the gateway to success. Cee-Lo's haziness about remembering whether or not he graduated is an allusion not only to his drug use—which is also critiqued in the track's chorus—but also to a working-class reading of education as not being a solution for Cee-Lo's socioeconomic condition. He struggles both economically and ethically— as a means of betterment, he considers drug dealing rather than pursuing a degree. He ultimately talks himself out of it, citing faith and spiritual awareness, a nod to the steady prominence of the southern black church.

Big Boi also raps about coming of age in Atlanta and the life lessons he learned, such as learning to smoke weed, pimping, and becoming a rapper. Particularly striking is Big Boi's self-categorization as "Rosemary's Baby," the spawn of Satan. This is a direct contrast to Cee-Lo's leaning toward faith. Moreover, "Rosemary's Baby" is a reference to being unwanted by his mother.[19] It is also an acknowledgment of his being a social and cultural outcast—both in the South and in hip-hop—which Big Boi navigates as difficult yet fruitful terrain. André picks up on Big Boi's intentions and ends the song with a harsh critique of voting, another cornerstone of civil rights rhetoric. André argues the uselessness of voting when the black politicians that run are "acting white"[20] and not pursuing André's best interests.

André also brings his verse full circle to connect with Cee-Lo's opening lyrics, stating he "never smelled the aroma of diploma."[21] Education and voting rights, a reflection of a functioning democratic space, are dismissed as avenues of socioeconomic progress. This dismissal is intentional, as both OutKast and Cee-Lo are breaking away from the heraldry of the civil rights movement to carve out space to articulate the newer challenges and realities of being young, southern, and black while pushing to be upwardly mobile. Perry writes, "Despite the undemocratic means of dealing with those not imagined to reside within the framework of normalcy, the status of an OutKast is celebrated. The implication here is that the critical gaze provided by otherness, that greater sense of reality by the epistemological advantages of otherness . . . makes being an outcast worthwhile."[22] The members of OutKast position themselves between two parallel renderings of democracy: the irony of southern black folks' upholding the purity of democracy as an idealistic access to better life and the counternarrative of democracy in the South as a threat to their very existence. OutKast's recognition of not only their marginalization but also their refusal to acknowledge that the South does move on after 1968 is significant in using their musical catalog as a blueprint for updating why the hip-hop South is introspective and reflective of how young blacks exist at the sharp intersections of expected performance, idealistic longing, and jarring realities of the contemporary American South.

This reckoning is amplified at the 1995 Source Awards, where OutKast pushes past the geographic and cultural boundaries of the region or "southness" into the experimental and metacultural possibilities of southern black expression. The Source Awards' dominantly New York audience, in addition to their booing, jolts the ear and affirms hip hop's hyperregional focus in the early to mid-1990s. The booing crowd identifies hip-hop as northeastern, urban, and rigidly masculine, an aesthetic that was a daunting task for non-northeastern performers to try to break through. Even for celebrated West Coast artists like Snoop Dogg, who menacingly and repeatedly asked the crowd "You don't love us?" during the show indicated the challenge of being recognized—and respected— by northeast hip-hop enthusiasts. That night in 1995 proved to be the climax of the conflict instigated by both West Coast Death Row Records and East Coast Bad Boy Records, the bitter lyrical and personal battle between Tupac Shakur and Notorious B.I.G., and OutKast, a southern act, chosen as "Best New Rap Group." The crowd's increasingly despondent sonic rejection of hip-hop outside of New York foregrounds the premise for reading OutKast's acceptance speech as blatant and unforgiving southern black protest, a rallying cry for forcefully creating space for the hip-hop South to come into existence.

Christopher "Kid" Reid and Salt-N-Pepa presented OutKast their award. Upbeat and playful, Kid said, "Ladies help me out" to announce the winner, but there is a distinctive drop in their enthusiasm when they name OutKast the winner of the category. The inflection in their voices signifies shock and even disappointment, as Kid quickly tries to be diplomatic by shouting out OutKast's frequent collaborators and label mates Goodie Mob. The negative reaction from the crowd was immediate, sharp and continuous booing.

Big Boi starts his acceptance speech, dropping a few colloquial words immediately recognizable as *proper* hip-hop—"word" and "what's up?"

Over a growingly irritated crowd, Big Boi acknowledges being in New York, "y'all's city," and tries to show respect to the New York rappers by crediting them as "original emcees." Big Boi recognizes he is an outsider, his southern drawl long and clear in his pronunciation of "south" as "souf," yet he attempts to be diplomatic and respectful of New York. There is also a recognition that where he is from, Atlanta, is also a city: his term, "y'all's city," is not only a recognition of his being an outsider but a proclamation that he, too, comes from a city—except it is a different city. Big Boi's embrace of Atlanta as urban challenges previous cultural narratives of southerners as incapable of maneuvering within an urban setting. Because of a long-standing and comfortable assumption that the American South was incapable of anything urban—such as mass transit, tall buildings, bustling neighborhoods and other interchangeable forms of communities—beliefs about southerners' perspectives remained aligned with rural, read as is, "country" and "backward," sensibilities incapable of functioning in an urban cultural setting. These sensibilities often played out in longhand form via literature or in popular black music, with a focus on dialect and language standing in as a signifier of regional and cultural distinction.

Consider Rudolph Fisher's southern protagonist, King Solomon Gillis, from the 1925 short story *City of Refuge*. Fisher characterizes Gillis, a black man from rural North Carolina, as naive and awestruck not only about New York but about city life in general. As the story opens, Fisher describes Gillis's ride on the subway as "terrifying," with "strange and terrible sounds."[23] References to the bang and clank of the subway doors and the close proximity of each train as "distant thunder" are particularly striking, a subtle sonic nod to Gillis's rural southernness and his inability to articulate the subway system outside of his limited southern experiences.[24] The references to "heat," "oppression," and "suffocation" also suggest southern weather as well as a belief about the American South as an unending repetition of slavery and its effects.[25]

It is important to point out that Gillis certainly is not a fearful man in the literal sense: he migrated to Harlem out of necessity and desperation, in fear of being lynched after shooting a white man back home. Yet Fisher's attention to sound positions Gillis as an outsider. Further, Fisher describes Gillis as "Jonah emerging from the whale," a biblical allusion to triumph over a difficult situation and a reference to rebirth, the possibility of a new life and new purpose.[26] This can be associated with the biblical reckoning of southern black folks migrating out of the South to seek socioeconomic change and advancement. Still, the transition of southern black folks to life in the city is not easy: Gillis's train ride symbolizes the move from one difficult landscape to another. Although Gillis is ultimately confronted with the brutality he was trying to avoid in North Carolina, his repeated proclamation, "They even got cullud policemans!" amplifies his southernness and naiveté.[27] Fisher's intentional use of written-out dialect and the repetitiveness of Gillis's awe of seeing black police officers blot out the characteristic of region but not white supremacy. Gillis's acceptance of black police officers blurs the binaries of the Great Migration as a testament to black folks looking for socioeconomic change outside of the American South, a terror-ridden space for blacks. It also suggests, however, the unfortunate anxiety of those who decide to remain in the South, complacent in the lack of social equality.

Seventy years later, Big Boi as a Georgian returns to New York with the confidence of both rural and southern sensibilities outside of the immediately recognizable urban trope that is embodied in New York. Big Boi's full embrace of being "cullud," in both the linguistic and cultural elements that Fisher's longhand dialect represented as authentic southernness, is jarring because his intentional embrace of southern blackness as othered anchors his approach to rap music. Big Boi does not posture the South as a space or place in need of escape or reposturing. Rather, the hyperawareness from both Big Boi and André in front of the predominantly New York crowd ruptures the accepted narrative of the South as needing saving by nonsouthern counterparts. Big Boi's speech forces the audience to deromanticize its notions of northeastern supremacy and recognize the South as capable of hip-hop. Their direct booing is a sonic representation of that discomfort.

From this perspective, André's now iconic remarks in their acceptance speech further emphasized Big Boi's departure from reckoning with northeastern hip-hop as the standard. He stumbles in his speech, possibly because of nerves or irritation, and, like Big Boi, must talk over the crowd. André talks about having the "demo tape and don't nobody wanna hear it," a double signifier of being rejected for his southernness and the difficulty of breaking into the music industry. André's frustration with being unheard as a southerner can also be extended into the actual production of the tape by OutKast's production team Organized Noize, who drew from southern musical influences like funk, blues, and gospel to ground their beats. André's call to arms, "The south got something to say," rallied other southern rappers to self-validate their music. It is important to note that André's rally called to the entire South, not just Atlanta. This is significant in thinking about southern experiences as nonmonolithic, the aural-cultural possibilities of multiple Souths and their various intersections using hip-hop aesthetics.

OutKast moves past their rejection at the Source Awards via their second album *ATLiens* (Atlanta aliens), which offered an equal rejection of hip-hop culture's binaries. The album's use of otherworldly sonic signifiers, such as synthesizers and pockets of silence that sound like space travel, embodied their deliberate isolation from mainstream hip-hop culture and the beginnings of Stankonia, or the hip-hop South.

Book Overview

I borrow the term "Stankonia" from the title of OutKast's 2000 album *Stankonia* to frame my articulation of a hip-hop South. Stankonia can be read as southern dialect for "stank on ya" or as a useful metaphor to speak the messy truth—stank—of contemporary southern black identity to power. I engage OutKast's body of work as a point of departure for understanding how post–civil rights southerners excavate spaces of imagination, possibility, and cultural influences as they fold onto each other in a complex present. The significance of OutKast's work is twofold: it is the reclamation of southern black identity in the present and a counterpoint to the historical and linear descriptions of southernness as racially rigid and fixated on its traumatic past without consideration of the present.

Chapter 1 is dedicated to how OutKast moves past southness, southern experiences hinged on the American South as a physical location, into southernness, the sociocultural conceptualization of southern life without the restrictions of regional affiliation. I argue that OutKast's intentional dismount from a standardized national hip-hop narrative that highlights bicoastal experiences and discourses destabilizes hip-hop's position as an expression only of bicoastal black modernity. Instead, they use hip-hop as a point of departure for contemporary southern black performance, not necessarily its totality.

Chapter 2 is an analysis of Kiese Laymon's use of southern hip-hop aesthetics as a form of storytelling in his 2013 debut novel *Long Division*. The novel focuses on a young boy named City who attempts to navigate his racial identity as a time traveler via a hole in the ground near his house in post-Katrina Mississippi. In addition to his reference to OutKast's song "Aquemini" as an epithet for the novel, Laymon's attention to young southern black boys and girls and how they interact is reminiscent of parts 1 and 2 of "Da Art of Storytellin'," also on the *Aquemini* album. Further, *Long Division* engages questions of southern blackness in the past and present by teasing out the messy intersections of two pivotal moments of southern black identity: Freedom Summer and Hurricane Katrina via storytelling and hip-hop. Like OutKast, Laymon's storytelling leans heavily on the construction of blurred temporal lines of southern black identity and generational anxiety about what it means to be free and love freely.

Based on hip-hop, chapter 3 offers a symbiotic analysis of slavery and its representations in contemporary popular culture such as the television series *Underground*, Quentin Tarantino's film *Django Unchained*, and Edward P. Jones's *The Known World*. I argue that these texts use hip-hop aesthetics to create an imaginary South that forays into how slavery is revisited in contemporary black culture. I maintain that these representations serve as a case study of slavery's position in a hip-hop South by illustrating how black oppression, black complicity, and black protest remain inextricably linked.

Chapter 4 is an interrogation of the southern hip-hop space, "the trap" using the music of Clifford "T.I." Harris and the Mississippi author Jesmyn Ward's books *Where the Line Bleeds* and *Men We Reaped*. In southern hip-hop, the trap signifies not only an illicit but nihilistically masculine space. It sonically and lyrically reflects the socioeconomic disparities that plague working-class Atlanta communities. Specifically, I use Ward's writing and Harris's complex narration of trap rap—that is, the fragmentation of his performance personas as the polished and Hollywood ready "T.I." and the other his drug dealer persona T.I.P.—to position the trap as a mourning space where young southern black men's grief is made legible.

Ultimately, *Chronicling Stankonia* situates OutKast's reckoning with the contemporary American South as theoreticians and not just as cultural producers. OutKast repositions black people as central to the complexities of the southern sociohistorical landscape. Similarly, I intend to demonstrate that the contemporary black American South is capable of its own recognition and critical insight outside the mainstream narrative that favors whitewashed accounts of southern identities rather than appreciating the full-bodied realities that dictate how and why contemporary southernness owes much of its buoyancy to its black communities.

ONE: THE DEMO TAPE AIN'T NOBODY WANNA HEAR

While most people consider the biggest takeaway from OutKast's historic win at the 1995 Source Awards to be André Benjamin's iconic declaration "the South got something to say," the opening of Benjamin's acceptance speech is also a theorization of the black South's rough transition into bicoastal hip-hop and contemporary American culture at large.[1] Sonically and visibly frustrated, Benjamin starts his speech: "It's like this though. I'm tired of close-minded folks, you know what I'm saying? . . . We got this demo tape and don't nobody wanna hear it." On the surface, Benjamin's statement suggests a familiar narrative in hip-hop: "We tryna make it and nobody would give us a chance but we made it anyway." However, Benjamin also invokes the regional biases of hip-hop, especially by New York City artists and record labels, citing their refusal to listen to OutKast's music—or to celebrate their win—as antisouthernness. New York's rejection of OutKast by booing and showing disinterest sonically and culturally signified OutKast's moniker as southern hip-hop rejects, taking root in northeast hip-hop's inability to literally listen and make legible OutKast's contemporary southernness.

I argue that Benjamin's belief that "the South got something to say" is the genesis point for the hip-hop South, but his statement that OutKast is the creator of an unheard and disrespected demo tape is an articulation of the group's subversion of rejection into an aesthetic. It is the beginning of what would pull through OutKast's growing body of work: an incessant need to experiment with their southern blackness and expand notions of the black South past physical boundaries and the limited imaginations of nonsoutherners within and outside of hip-hop. In their discography, both Benjamin and Patton center being "OutKasted" as a working verb, a constant experiment of creative evolution and dabbling in world and culture building. Their music transitions the South from its physical limitations into a cultural concept, poking and prodding at the ways the South intersects with the identities, memories, experiences, and possibilities of black people. OutKast is an unabashed cultural investigation of black southernness that bows to nothing but the group's own prowess. Ultimately, their work pursues the breaking of limitations about the South as a viable and vibrant space of creative reckoning with the past, present, and future.

Are You ATLien(s)?

If *Southernplayalisticadillacmuzik* is an introduction to contemporary Atlanta and southern hip-hop, OutKast's second studio album *ATLiens* (1996) is an amplified response to their rejection at the Source Awards. Because OutKast's centering of a southern sociocultural landscape did not and could not fully take root in the hip-hop narrative of the moment—the growing animosity between East and West Coast hip-hop communities and their differing approaches to urbanity-as-authenticity took center stage—*ATLiens* moves far into the future to think through the implications of hip-hop and agency in the post–civil rights South. The album's simultaneous focus on the past—both recent and longer-standing—and present demonstrates what Alondra Nelson refers to as "past-future visions."[2] *ATLiens* creates a fantastic account of the migration of southern blackness on its own terms: an envisioning of the South's future as a polytemporal space of past and present experiences. The album can be read as a speculative reimagining of a new migration, akin to the early twentieth-century phenomenon, that focuses on the black folks who *stayed* in the South. Instead of moving to the romanticized Northeast, OutKast imagines what would happen if black southerners moved past historical boundaries into the speculative space that could house their otherness—outer space.

ATLiens carves space for OutKast's imagining of the hip-hop South as a possibility of futurity, pulling from historical and futuristic black aesthetics that speak to their hybridized experiences of being Southern, black, and invested in hip-hop.[3] What I mean here is that OutKast was already dabbling in ideas of ascension on *Southernplayalisticadillacmuzik* that would be more fleshed out on *ATLiens*. For example, the track "D.E.E.P." from *Southernplayalisticadillacmuzik* is the first introduction to OutKast as aliens. The song opens with the lines, "Greetings, Earthlings. Take me to your leader."[4] The greeting, stiff and roboticized, sonically amplifies the popular treatment of aliens in science fiction as othered and even monstrous, a stark opposition to (white) normalcy. In this sense, the alien's greeting is both a salutation and a challenge: the alien is asking about Earth's leadership and OutKast is responding with a searing narrative of paranoia and antiestablishment, promising both physical and psychological retorts of violence for devaluing their existence and insight. On "D.E.E.P.," Patton and Benjamin do not shy away from the very real crises on Earth and especially in the South, referencing the AIDS epidemic, poverty, and white supremacy. The challenge to "go deep" is multilayered when grounded in hip-hop as a tool of social commentary. On the surface, OutKast asks the audience—symbolized by the alien—if they are sure they want to go deeper in listening to two southern rappers who are not fixated on the stereotypical ideas of southern blacks as backward and slow. OutKast raps about their endangered state from a southern perspective, aligning their own status as outsiders with the alien.

The appearance of an alien greeting listeners at the beginning of the track "Two Dope Boyz in a Cadillac" on the *ATLiens* album is an extension of OutKast's full embrace of their moniker and experimenting with notions of southern black essentialisms. The "alien" introduced here can be read as Patton and Benjamin's introducing themselves as "alien" and separate from bicoastal hip-hop. *ATLiens* is a concept album that captures the widely recognizable trope of racial displacement and repurposes it to speak to their alienation from hip-hop as southerners. The creation of "ATLiens"—natives to the city of Atlanta but also alien to those who view the city and the South as alien or foreign—is rooted firmly in a long line of southern-influenced funk artists who used space to establish self-autonomy (such as Sun-Ra, or frequent OutKast collaborator George Clinton). *ATLiens* is an experiment not only in OutKast's shift in the way they aligned themselves with hip-hop but also in the evolution of their views of how their southernness could be manifested in their music. To build on a theory offered by my former student Jeff Wallace, *ATLiens* is suggestive of the beginning of OutKast's hip-hop odyssey: the introduction, a prelude titled "You May Die," is the beginning of OutKast's journey into space, a departure from the binding parameters of Earth, the southeast United States, and hip-hop. The track suggests that there is risk in leaving the familiar, but the reward is self-autonomy. The following track, "Two Dope Boyz in a Cadillac," is OutKast's arrival, a subversion of the alien visiting them from "D.E.E.P." Their bodies, like their music, are made mobile via the Cadillac, now a spaceship that falls into the musical lineage of funk artists like George

Clinton and Parliament-Funkadelic's "mothership." The imagery of OutKast's reimagined mothership pulls from the past and present, signifying upon the slave ship that brought black people to OutKast's original homeland of the South and the trope of the funk mothership that would bring black folks and their southern sensibilities to space, the final "homeland" of infinite freedom and autonomy outside of white supremacy. The track following "Two Dope Boyz," "ATLiens," affirms this by asking listeners to "throw their hands in the air" if they like "fish and grits and all that pimp shit," examples of southern culture they introduced on *Southernplayalisticadillacmuzik*.[5] This track title, like the rest of the album, solidifies and celebrates OutKast's self-imposed exclusion and freedom from the world.

In OutKast's imagination, the black South was no longer physically confined to the lower end of the United States. *ATLiens* demonstrates the South as fluid and mobile. This is most visibly demonstrated in the liner notes, which take the form of a comic book designed under the guidance of D. L. Warfield. On the cover, an illustrated OutKast is seen squared up in a fighting stance ready to battle against a backdrop of neon-colored villains as (anti)heroes. The comic itself, written by OutKast and Big Rube, is a roughly scripted battle of good and evil against the evil musical force called Nosamulli. It captures the materialization of OutKast's rejection of bicoastal hip-hop rules. The *ATLiens* comic book visualizes the dirtiness of southern hip-hop and the sliding scale of time and unbound possibilities of southern identity and experience. The South as an otherworldly place pivots on the infinite possibility of time and the existence of outer space as parallel to the uncontainable and ever refreshing reservoir of southern time and memory.

OutKast's intentional disembodiment from bicoastal hip-hop creates room for larger discussions of race, class, and identity that remain connected to past southern identities. For example, Patton's superpower is the ability to transform into a black panther. From a historical perspective, the black panther symbolized the Lowndes County Freedom Organization in Hayneville, Alabama, before its more recognizable attachment to the Black Panther Party coming out of Oakland, California.[6] Additionally, in Marvel comics the Black Panther is the superhero identity of T'Challa, the king of a fictitious African country named Wakanda. Adilifu Nama's study *Super Black* contextualizes T'Challa as a global southern hero, "an idealized composite of third-world black revolutionaries and the anticolonialist movement of the 1950s they represented."[7] Nama labels T'Challa as "a recurperative figure and majestic signifier of the best of the black anticolonialist movement."[8] Patton's superpower as a black panther situates him in the larger sociocultural context of freedom and struggle associated with the South and the African diaspora. The comic book allows OutKast to refurbish their narratives of southernness associated with Atlanta while pushing past the boundaries of blackness and identity to tap into a larger global black experience. Although other hip-hop artists such as A Tribe Called Quest, Snoop Dogg, MF Doom, and GZA also use the comic-book aesthetic in their liner notes, OutKast uses the comic book as a distinguishing tool of southern agency and figurative being in hip-hop culture. The *ATLiens* comic book provides an interstitial space between oral tradition—a prominent form of remembrance in the South—and hard print for OutKast's imaginative exploits to exist.

Further, OutKast signifies on the comic book as a contemporary talking-book, the trope Henry Louis Gates theorizes in *The Signifying Monkey* as a "double-voiced text that talks to other texts."[9] The *ATLiens* comic book is a double-voiced text in multiple registers: it represents the literal voice of Patton and Benjamin, it can be read as a tangible manifestation of OutKast's awareness of themselves as southern black men (aligning with Du Bois's theorization of double consciousness), and the comic-book form bridging hip-hop into broader areas and audiences of popular culture through the lens of regionalism.

Consider the music video for *ATLiens*'s first single "Elevators." The video opens with the sounds of a pan flute and strings and shows a group of people wading through a dense forest led by OutKast. The shot then pans to a young Asian boy sitting under a tree reading the *ATLiens* comic book. A sample of the track's sparse accompaniment of bass kicks, a wood block, and high hats softly plays in the background, signifying the talking drum and the announcement of an arrival. The boy's eyes widen in interest and possibly amazement, while the video transitions into the beginning of the comic book set in a classroom and on a graduation stage for Benjamin's opening verse.

Benjamin raps about his own humble beginnings while sneaking into the classroom in a black turban and purple tie-dyed shirt. Visibly bored and irritated, the scene then shifts to Benjamin's graduation, where he is now in a glowing white cap and gown. The rest of his classmates don dark blue caps and gowns, booing him as he dances across the stage. This scene is significant because it is a visual interpretation of Benjamin's being booed at the Source Awards: Benjamin's purple tie-dyed shirt symbolizes the same-colored dashiki he wore at the Source Awards and the video classmates stand in for the New Yorkers who booed him offstage. Benjamin's white cap and gown represent a physical rendering of his own "graduation" from standardized hip-hop. The classroom scene for Benjamin's verse is also a visual testament of his verse from "Git Up, Git Out," the track on which he questions the long-standing southern black mantra of formal education as the (only) path to success.

Waiting outside for Benjamin is Patton in a Cadillac, doubly symbolic of the Cadillac as a literal vehicle of southern upward mobility as well as the mothership/future, waiting to take Benjamin and Patton home. As Patton finishes his verse, he and Benjamin get out of the car and walk toward and into their destiny. A wrecking ball demolishes the car and the video transitions into a dimly lit undisclosed location where Benjamin reads and Patton "preaches" to a group of listeners. They are also seen burning incense and smoking a hookah before the video turns back to the opening scene of the video with Benjamin and Patton leading a group through a jungle. They are on high alert and quickly usher their caravan of followers to keep moving forward as they flee from an unseen evil force. The group makes it to their final destination, a landscape possibly signifying upon the Rastafarian promised land of Zion and a subversion of the biblical Canaan. Children are seen running toward the pyramids as the camera pans to black figures walking around the pyramids and greeting each other. Benjamin and Patton's eyes glow green in acknowledgment, a physical sign of being an OutKast and alien finally returning home.

The concluding scenes of the "Elevators" music video shows the intersection of multiple threads representing black people's constant search for home, belonging, and their future selves. It is important to note that in the second half of the video—the journey to home—Benjamin and Patton are parallel to the conductors of the historical Underground Railroad. They are slowly and cautiously moving a group of outcasts through the wilderness to a place of freedom while running from patrollers—akin to slave patrollers—who are hunting them down. The patrollers look for hidden—illegible—signs using infrared vision to make the runaway group's whereabouts visible. This futuristic tracking method alludes to the past–present futurity of slavery's long-reaching residual effects tinged with science fiction, particularly the allusions to the *Predator* film series. With nods toward imagery and the lore of the Underground Railroad and slavery, Rastafarian-influenced imagery of spirituality as a counter to white Christianity, and the pilgrimage of self-discovery, the "Elevators" video presents evidence of OutKast's use of *ATLiens* as initial efforts in world-building as a form of legacy that centers on and celebrates the agency of southern black people.

When the Heroes Eventually Die: *Aquemini*

OutKast's third album, *Aquemini* (1998), is a masterful work showcasing the group's reflection on their legacy as black southerners and their growth as artists. The name, a mash-up of Patton and Benjamin's astrological signs, carries on the group's aspirations to be both futuristic and experimental. *Aquemini* also highlights the group's maturation as men and as artists in control of their craft. This is most clearly reflected in the album's production: the group's own production efforts are more prominent on the album *Aquemini* with the majority of production credit going to OutKast and their production partner and DJ David "Mr. DJ" Sheats. *Aquemini* is not OutKast's first attempt at producing: OutKast and Sheats also produced songs on the *ATLiens* album, including the critically acclaimed hit "Elevators." *Aquemini* takes full advantage of Organized Noize's tutelage: live instrumentation and funk influences float throughout the album. The sonic depth of the album parallels the lyrical prowess, offering a sonic genealogy of both nostalgia and change. Although still evolving as artists—Benjamin especially reaches new heights in his lyricism—*Aquemini* is also a sonic memoir, a review of defining moments from their pasts and expectations for their future.

The album delicately balances nostalgia for the past and embrace of the uncertain future. For example, "Return of the G" showcases Benjamin and Patton's personal growth: Benjamin emphasizes that he feels "better than ever" after coming fully into his own sense of self and purpose as a first-time father, and Patton echoes similar sentiments about embracing fatherhood and wanting to do better for his then toddler daughter. Both men acknowledge that they have grown since their 1994 arrival in hip-hop. Yet "Return of the G" is also a warning to their fans and listeners that their personal growth is not a deterrent to their equally growing talents as rappers. Benjamin's opening verse is especially critical about being compared to his younger self and about the rumors swirling around his personal life choices. It is significant that "Return of the G" is the first full-length track on the album as it sets a precedent for the ways Benjamin and Patton are reconfiguring how to be OutKast while maintaining their fan base.

The title track "Aquemini" reemphasizes the duo's introspection throughout the album, affirming their love and support of one another even through inevitable change. The track opens with the song's chorus, a stirring statement about mortality and loyalty. They rap:

> Even the sun goes down, heroes eventually die
> Horoscopes often lie and sometimes "why"
> Nothin' is for sure, nothing is for certain, nothin' last forever
> But until they close the curtain
> It's him and I Aquemini.[10]

They are aware that change impacts every part of life, even the one constant of life on Earth, the sun. This also a subtle acknowledgment of their status as ATLiens, and their "return" to Earth and witnessing of its mortality. Mortality threads through the next line about heroes and their deaths. Although "Aquemini" does not directly name a particular figure, the casual description of a hero's death, especially the use of the word "eventually," is tinged with southern sensibilities. The South is known for holding tight to its heroes of the past. In the black South, the heroes are like phoenixes, resuscitated as myths and legends instead of actual people. Their myths are romantic and infinite, passed down between generations. Therefore, this opening line is as socially and historically loaded as it is speculative: "heroes" here is subversive, it deflates the blind and often uncritical adoration of black folks and their leaders in order to break new ground to consider the South and its futurities from a refreshed perspective. If "heroes" is read here as the prominent figures of the civil rights era, their physical and mythological deaths are necessary for the South to move forward. Colloquially, death is not the end but the beginning. The opening of Patton's verse speaks to the need for new myths and stories, resituating the civil rights iconography of a bus away from Rosa Parks and the Montgomery bus boycott to Spike Lee's 1995 film *Get On the Bus*. Particularly striking in Patton's reframing of the bus trope using Lee is the emphasis on young black men and their journey to change. When Patton raps "now is the time to get on," this is both the physical action of boarding a bus and a southern euphemism meaning to go away or move forward. The updating of the bus trope as a marker of physical mobility and cultural change signifies upon its lasting importance in southern black communities across generations.

Additionally, if the heroes referenced in "Aquemini" is OutKast referring to themselves, then the "death" of their former art and personas is making room for new art and new identities—that is, the rise of Benjamin's persona "André 3000." Although "André 3000" will not fully manifest until Benjamin introduces himself as such on the Louisiana native

Mystikal's 1999 song "Neck Uv Da Woods," Benjamin speaks to his multifaceted personas on *Aquemini* under the guise of being a member of the astrological sign Gemini. On the "Aquemini" track, Benjamin's verses are delivered in distinctive ways, the first verse being sonically somber and empathetic, alluding to the lasting terror of the Atlanta child murders (in 1979–1981) and the loss of childhood innocence that the murders embodied. Benjamin refers to the murdered children in the present tense, creating the haunting image that somehow, somewhere, they were still on their way to the candy lady, a staple figure in working-class black communities that sold candy, ice cream, and other treats to local children.

Benjamin's voice is soft if not tender when referencing the victims of the murders. Further, he delicately walks a line of innocence between nostalgia and childhood terror—blending the imagery of the candy lady and the palpable fear felt black children. Benjamin's voice is used to speak for the children never found and still living—remembered—in his verses. He then apologizes for drifting to the past, switching his focus to articulations of being misidentified and labeled in the present. Although apologetic for drifting between the past and present, Benjamin again revisits the past in terms of righteousness and protest and how the past is literally and culturally dressed. He simultaneously discredits the upholding of sartorial respectability politics long-held in the South while critiquing the belief in sartorial disrespectability of (southern) hip-hop culture—dreadlocks and gold grills (teeth).

Benjamin's second verse on "Aquemini" is delivered more forcefully and confidently, under the guise of "André Ben" the sonic twin of his previous delivery as André Benjamin. In this verse, Benjamin celebrates his Africanness—"original skin"—and his alienness/outkastedness. He states his mind "warps and bends" meaning, is in constant flux between ideas, time periods, and experiences, and is a complicated being. Before returning to the chorus, André addresses the performances of both his personas, saying, "Ya'll just gone have to make amends." Benjamin's last line is Du Boisian: Benjamin is hyperaware of not only the twoness of being Gemini but also of being southern and black.

Whereas Benjamin is critically nostalgic—using the past to complicate the state of the present—Patton is more embracing and celebratory of the past in tracks like "West Savannah," a homage to his hometown, and his verse about his sexual coming-of-age on "SpottieOttieDopalicious" and "Da Art of Storytellin' (Part 1)." Combining their two approaches to the past and future creates a track like "Da Art of Stoytellin' (Part 2)," where they hypothesize about writing the last rhyme on Earth before the apocalypse. Benjamin talks about society's horrific past treatment of the environment and the physical markers of the end of the world. Instead of cowering in fear, Benjamin dials up "the Dungeon"—the basement of Organized Noize producer Rico Wade's family home, where OutKast and other members of the Dungeon Family got their start—to record the final song on Earth. Benjamin's return to the Dungeon is a play on the euphemism of calling it home. The Dungeon is the center of the world that Benjamin has come to know and will hold significant meaning as a foreshadowing of Out-Kast's following album *Stankonia*.

Patton is also en route to the Dungeon, his family in tow and battling visions of the apocalypse: that is, the Four Horsemen. The end of the world is made real to Patton through a very southern sensibility—he noticed the lack of people sitting on their front porches—a central meeting place for southerners. After writing and laying down the final verse—literally and figuratively—Patton describes the final beat as "dirty" and distorted, a line akin to last words and Patton's eulogizing hip-hop using southern aesthetics. The final chorus, "All is well, nothing's well," is sung by a deep and throaty chorus of echoing voices, alluding to the voice of God as the final sound the audience hears before the world dies (the track ends).[11]

The remaining three tracks on *Aquemini* are grouped together in a powerful way, a triad of freedom songs that showcase OutKast's changing definition of freedom. These tracks, "Nathaniel," "Liberation," and "Chonkyfire," offer insight into Patton and Benjamin's personal, industrial, and social grappling with what it means to be free. "Nathaniel," an interlude and freestyle recorded over the phone by a then incarcerated friend of Patton and Sheats named Nathaniel. A biting criticism of the prison industrial complex and the difficulties of being an incarcerated black man, Nathaniel's freestyle compares prison to slavery and tries to stay positive in a space filled with desperation. Hip-hop is his saving grace, emphasizing his desire to be as free as his verse and using rap as a tool that allows him to speak his truth to power. It is important to note that Nathaniel's freestyle is not redemptive in the sense that he is remorseful for his actions. Rather, his freestyle is a story of his own making, an effort to establish his own agency and claim himself in a system that is oppressing him.

Nathaniel's interlude leads into the song "Liberation," a collaborative effort with fellow members of the Dungeon Family Cee-Lo Green, Big Rube, Joi, and the honorary member Erykah Badu. The song opens with a soft piano medley, chimes, and a prominent rainstick. Benjamin's verse opens the song, metaphorically comparing the freedom of self-autonomy as a "thin line" that can teeter when one loses self-confidence. Freedom is the ability to make one's own choices—a prominent trope in Benjamin's verses—without fearing judgment. Patton rhymes next, addressing freedom as a privilege to give back to those who helped him to be successful. Cee-Lo's verse is particularly striking in its sermonic delivery, defining freedom as the ability to overcome struggle. Sonically, Cee-Lo's squall bridges the past and present: his moaning and holler are sonically reminiscent of Negro spirituals and songs sung at church revivals. Freedom is a spiritual experience. Cee-Lo references both the biblical story of Noah's ark and the African American folktale of "If the People Could Fly," a story of slaves emancipating themselves by using a secret word that lets them fly away to freedom. Cee-Lo's verse suggests that grit and optimism are in tandem with freedom as a form of perseverance. Erykah Badu's verse is a cautionary tale about what freedom is not. She takes on the persona of a budding artist facing the temptations of newfound fame. Badu criticizes the downfalls behind the glamour of the music industry and points out the consequences of success such as the loss of friends and corruption of artistic vision. Badu thus offers up freedom as the maintenance of sanity and artistic purity while being commercially successful, a challenge that Badu shares with both Patton and Benjamin.

Aquemini's final track on the album, "Chonkyfire," is a spectacular way to end a memoiresque album. It is a hazy, electric guitar-riff-filled celebration of OutKast's journey, affirming their music as akin to the pied piper in being able to lure fans out of their homes and dens of comfort. It is possible to read OutKast's likening to the pied piper as part of a final calling out of northeast hip-hoppers, a begrudging moment of reckoning for hip-hop's stubborn purists to recognize how the South is changing hip-hop permanently. Even more fittingly, OutKast samples their rejection at the 1995 Source Awards, a final sonic marker of how they had come as artists and that hip-hop's bicoastal aesthetics failed to shut down their creativity as southern artists. After the sample of being booed, the song's accompaniment slows down to a crawl, a nod to the Texas aesthetic of screw music and the nonmonolithic nature of southern hip-hop. The end of "Chonkyfire" sounds like a dying tape, a sonic indicator of both the end of the album and a final salute to OutKast's assertion of their own will.

Live from the Center of the New Earth/South: *Stankonia*

With their fourth studio album, *Stankonia* (2000), OutKast is what southern folks call "good and grown": they are in full control of their creative process and also masters of their southern performative domain. Sonically, *Stankonia* demonstrates the prowess of OutKast and David Sheats as a self-sustaining production team—Earthtone III—outside of Organized Noize's influence. For example, the album demonstrates influences of electronic dance music (EDM), heavy metal, gospel, and reggae in addition to their initial influences of funk. *Stankonia*, a phonetic spelling of the phrase "stank on ya," epitomizes OutKast's continued revision of contemporary southern black narratives using hip-hop. Stankonia is a world all of its own, one that makes the black American South a conceptual yet tangible place where black identities and southernness fluidly intersect and overlap. A prominent trope on this album is "stank," the musty, less-than-savory, and (mis)pronounced aspects of black southern life. "Stank on ya" sonically illustrates OutKast's comfort, if not thriving, in the taboo and the mis-fitted pockets of hip-hop and American popular culture. Returning to the song "Da Art of Storytellin' (Part 2)" from *Aquemini*, Benjamin and Patton describe creating the last rhyme the world will ever hear. The Dungeon is the center of the Earth. *Stankonia* opens with Benjamin (now performing under the moniker André 3000), delivering a hazy, dispatch-esque introduction ("Live, from the center of the Earth"), where he lures the listener into Stankonia as a place "seven light years below sea level . . . the place from which all funky things come."[12] Stankonia is an extension of the music OutKast produced at the end of "Da Art Storytellin' (Part 2)." The Dungeon (Family) and southern hip-hop survive the apocalypse and form the root for starting a new world. Stankonia does not randomly appear. Rather, it is the result of a calculated investment in how the past, present, and future coexist to signify the complexity of southern blackness. A woman's moans vibrate across low synthesizers reminiscent of a zither, a sonic allusion that Stankonia is unlike any other physical and metaphorical space in the world, albeit influenced by the latter's sonic intonations. The repetition of the phrase "bouncing . . . we're bouncing!" signifies OutKast's multilayered construction of temporality and self-identity: the literal bouncing of the listener to the music, the sexual innuendo of bouncing as sonically reified by the moaning woman, and bouncing between past, present, and future point to the reason that Stankonia needs to exist outside of the expected scripts of hip-hop and southernness. The "funk" of bouncing between expectation and self-fulfillment renders Stankonia as a viable space for multiple and overlapping identities and experiences influenced by but not the totality of historic scripts of southern blackness. Stankonia *is* the hip-hop/new black South. It is the mountaintop and a soundtrack to why the mountaintop ain't flat.

Consider the opening song, "Gasoline Dreams," the first full track on the *Stankonia* album. Equally hazy as the album's introduction but with wild and loud electric guitar riffs for good measure, "Gasoline Dreams" criticizes the corrupt and overly assuming position of the American Dream as universally accepted—and sustainable—by all black Americans. "Gasoline Dreams" is a biting reminder that the racial *and* economic mountaintop of equality is not flat or fully retained by post–civil rights blacks. The song's opening and chorus, yell-rapped by Benjamin, mocks the generalized construct of the American Dream as *everyone's* dream: "Don't everybody love the smell of gasoline? Well burn, motherfucka burn, American Dreams / Don't everybody like the taste of apple pie? / Well snap for your slice of life I'm tellin' ya why."[13] Akin to the southern sensibility that grounds their delivery, these lines can be read from multiple viewpoints. A broader context of the lyrics suggests the American Dream as an all-consuming dream that quickly burns out its pursuers. This configuration of the American Dream parallels African Americans' pursuit of inclusion, if not assimilation, into mainstream America.

Additionally, the violent metaphors in "Gasoline Dreams" align with the South's violent history, the act and imagery of burning serving as signifiers of past lynchings of black men and women in the South and beyond. This line from the track's chorus juxtaposes the idea of achieving success at the expense of (violently) oppressed communities. Benjamin calls his listeners to action. In this sense Stankonia becomes a space of refuge where disenfranchised people and communities can rectify their own narratives without losing sight of the challenges of being oppressed. The OutKast member Big Boi's verse is a rant against police racial profiling—a common sociohistorical problem in southern spaces—and the drug culture but can also be read as an adamant rejection of sociocultural rules that do not speak to his experiences.

If Stankonia is a scathing response to the American Dream, another striking instance of OutKast's intonation of inverting a common trope of black struggle is heard on the track "B.O.B." Although the song does not directly correlate with the turbulent history of Iraq, the song title and bursts of sound fold OutKast back into a global conversation about poverty and oppressive rule. "B.O.B." is a lyrical assault on the poor conditions of living in the southern (Atlanta) black working class.

Benjamin and Patton rhyme across an instrumental blend of bass and a church organ, inundating the listener's ear with agency and anger. The church organ is just as angry and explosive, with riffs and keys banged out loudly and in opposition to the soft accompaniment often heard in a church setting. "B.O.B" brazenly discusses those issues that are often reserved for "closet prayer" and silent suffering, floating it all on a pounding EDM and rave-inspired foundation. By heavily using the organ and church choir at the end of the track, which chants "Power music! Electric revival!" OutKast subverts and updates the trope of the celebrated black church revival, a gathering of church folk and the lost, and repurposes the church trope and its music to give a voice to the marginalized black working class.[14] The hybrid sound of "B.O.B." provides a space for the reclamation of a disenfranchised southern African American narrative that blends the suffering trope that mandates much of African American religion with current trends in cultural expression that are reflected in hip-hop. OutKast's construction and residency in Stankonia is a metaphysical space doubly used as a coping device for the socioeconomic and racial discrimination faced in the South and as a space for speaking truth to power. Stankonia is the hip-hop South because it intentionally uses trauma, storytelling, and history to function on its own terms.

A Quick Note of Separation:
Speakerboxxx/The Love Below

For OutKast's fifth album, *Speakerboxxx/The Love Below*, Benjamin and Patton deliver a joint album that solidifies the duo's ability to mutually coexist without losing sight of their increasingly distinctive creative processes. The album is significant for many reasons, including the lack of a promotional tour after its release and the absence of Organized Noize from the double album's production. *Speakerboxxx/The Love Below* signifies OutKast's full maturation as artists and producers. The experimentation with multiple musical genres heard on *Stankonia* comes full circle with *Speakerboxxx/The Love Below*. Additionally, for many nonsoutherners, *Speakerboxxx/The Love Below* is OutKast's breakthrough album. It earned international recognition and multiple awards including the 2004 "Album of the Year" Grammy. Because of the album's wide appeal, I think about it as a sonic and physical signifier of OutKast's synced but distinctive personalities: Patton's "album," *Speakerboxxx*, remains true to the duo's solid positioning within the southern hip-hop hybrid they established with their catalog. *Speakerboxxx* most aligns with OutKast's back catalog and Organized Noize influence: percussion, boasting hard percussions and lively horns, witty chorus taglines and skits. Songs like "The Way You Move," "Rooster," and "Bowtie" feature an enthusiastic Patton delivering lyrics about the joys and challenges of being a successful southern black man. Other songs like "Reset" hark back to songs like "Liberation" as both speak to the need to reaffirm and refresh one's self-autonomy. Still, there are tender moments on the album like Patton speaking to his son Bamboo in the "Bamboo" interlude where Bamboo performs the chorus of OutKast's single "The Whole World" as his father cheers him on. Overall, *Speakerboxxx* accentuates Patton's acclimation in hip-hop, his literal tenure in people's sound systems—such as car speakers and boomboxes—and also the promise of being unapologetically unfiltered—the triple *x* of the title. The triple *x* also suggests Patton's sexual and masculine bravado.

The Love Below, however, features an inquisitive and experimental Benjamin, filled with falsettos, singsong lyrics, and a keen focus on his innermost contemplations about the world and his place in it. The title and album can be read in multiple ways: the sexual innuendo of having "love below" or oral sex, Benjamin's unseen layers and apprehensions as a socially anxious performer, or a clever descriptor of his roots as a southerner. Intriguingly, Benjamin seldom raps on *The Love Below*, an intentional departure from the way he is expected to perform and present himself as a rapper. In effect, Benjamin's experimentation with falsetto and spoken word points to his artistic influences like Prince and Anita Baker. Perhaps most intriguingly, Benjamin's interrogation of love, pleasure, and commitment are filtered through women's voices and experiences. From skits like "Where Are My Panties?" to "She's Alive," a hybrid of music and sound bites from an interview with Benjamin's mother, Sharon Benjamin-Hodo, a single mother, about raising Benjamin. Even the eccentric track "Dracula's Wedding," featuring the singer and chef Kelis, makes room for Benjamin to question the parameters of commitment through Dracula's immortality while expanding on Benjamin's initial question of "foreva eva?" from the *Stankonia* single "Ms. Jackson."

In addition to its critical acclaim, *Speakerboxxx/The Love Below* set up OutKast's next foray: their single feature-length film *Idlewild*.

"You Ain't Say Nothing Slick to Can of Oil": *Idlewild* and the Hip-Hop South

OutKast's 2006 film *Idlewild* is set in the Great Depression South. *Idlewild* follows the lives of lifelong friends Rooster and Percival as played by Patton and Benjamin, respectively. Rooster is a bootlegger and club owner and Percival is a mortician. A nod to the now defunct African American vacation hub of Idlewild, Michigan, the memory of Idlewild as an entertainment capital for blacks is resuscitated and rescripted into the fictitious/imaginary town of Idlewild, Georgia.[15] Idlewild's transition from the upper Midwest to the rural South is striking as it blurs lines of history and cultural memory with performance, and situates itself in Stankonia as an equally conceptual and imaginary space. This is especially relevant in the sense that *Idlewild* is set in the Great Depression yet performs music by OutKast and other post–civil rights era performers like Macy Gray and Janelle Monáe.[16]

Idlewild hinges on sound as the medium for articulating a temporal black southernness situated within the music. Although the film is set during the Great Depression era in the South, it remains attached to the present via its soundtrack, a heavy sampling of the group's Grammy Award–winning double album *Speakerboxxx/The Love Below*. These collisions of blues and hip-hop, the sacred and secular, present the South as a fluid space. A prominent trope of the hybridization of hip-hop and the juke joint seen and heard onscreen is Rooster's club "Church." Church speaks to the continued presence of not only the aesthetics associated with the blues but also the remixing of blues aesthetics into the way southern rap identifies itself as a contemporary art form. The physical space of the Church juke joint also encapsulates the live performances of the film's score. The physical and aural presence of Church signifies it as a living jukebox or collection of popular and "throwback" music that represents the blended blues and hip-hop aesthetic in the South. Church embodies the overlap of racial-cultural memories of southernness and contemporary black performance. The tensions resulting from these blurred lines take place in both the music and the listening practices and memories associated with the music. Aside from a few new songs that cover the blues/hip-hop hybrid used for the film, *Idlewild* is a reflection of OutKast's previous catalog, especially tracks from *Speakerboxxx/The Love Below*.

Further, *Idlewild* highlights multiple entry points into the South as a rendering of past cultural work. The nature of the music is made anew as it is used in the film and resuscitates not only the familiarity with OutKast's previous catalog but the revamping of the South as a living space of cultural memory. The connection between the past and present takes place on the imaginative front, easing the hard lines drawn between notions of historical period and contemporary performance.

In one memorable scene, Percival, played by Benjamin, wakes up to a chaotic array of chiming clocks. Cuckoo clocks, dancing-couple clocks, miniature grandfather clocks, and alarm clocks simultaneously confront his sleep. Percival, however, appears unfazed. In addition to the chiming clocks the scene plays a few piano chords from the track "Chronomentrophobia," a song from the *Idlewild* soundtrack. The track's opening, a bass kick and solitary snare that signify a ticking clock, is heard in tandem with Benjamin giving the definition of chronomentrophobia—the fear of clocks and time. It also sets the stage for Benjamin's rap, a semi-autobiographical sketch where he teeters between differing forms of agency—social responsibility and responsibility to his dreams. Like Percival, Benjamin is very much aware of time ticking away and his physical limits. His rhymes become a cultural memory, however, that immortalizes him.

The harrowing audiovisual display of clocks paired with Benjamin's rap immediately suggests running out of time, a nod toward the dichotomy of life and death, and the age-old adage "time is precious" or "time and youth are wasted on the young." The rhyme also references Benjamin's character Percival and his job as a mortician. The multiple references to death, memory, and resurrection are prominent representations of Percival's position as a caretaker of the dead and southern black cultural expression. Benjamin/Percival's self-euology, a simplistic but stunning warning to those who are "wasting time," also stands as a record of living. However, the sonic and physical tangibility of the clocks also points to the prominence of time's fluidity as a trope articulating contemporary southern blackness. The use of the song to remember Benjamin doubly exists as a representation of how music, specifically hip-hop, contributes to the cyclical nature of southern culture.

Slammed Cadillac Doors: OutKast Revisits the Hip-Hop South

After a decade-long hiatus, OutKast commemorated their twentieth anniversary in hip-hop with a reunion tour.[17] The schedule consisted of forty musical festivals and concerts over the summer of 2014. While the reunion tour incited heated conversation over their playlist—whether audiences favored OutKast as a mainstream pop group following *Speakerboxxx/The Love Below* or as the group represented in their preceding catalog—OutKast remained in control of their performance. Aside from the playlist, their use of live instrumentation amplified their negotiation of southernness and a revisitation of the time they spent constructing a hip-hop-inspired contemporary black South. Their band consisted of the same artists who provided a significant chunk of the background instrumentals from their recorded catalog.

Horns Unlimited, the trumpet players on their "SpottieOttieDopalicious" track, the bass guitarist Debra Killings, and the background singers Keisha Jackson and Joi all participated in their tour. The instrumentalists and vocalists sonically convene to demonstrate the overlap of OutKast's past, present, and future body of work. Their revisitation of their catalog suggests OutKast's willingness to preserve the sonic component of their hip-hop narrative. Yet their live performances also promise the possibility of slight improvisation from the recording, adding new depth and complexity to the body of work already in place. The ability to sample their sonic pasts to create new space for understanding their current and future position makes OutKast's reunion tour simply spectacular.

An additional component of OutKast's mastery of their performance is their fashion choices. Benjamin's black-and-white-colored jumpsuits range in proverbial messages from introspective—"Sold Out"—to more whimsical and lighthearted, such as "Fruit Snack Addict."[18] Patton's ensembles also pull from Atlanta's hip-hop history, whether diamond-studded chains and watches or plays on the Atlanta Braves jersey and other city paraphernalia. Patton's Atlanta fashion statements signify his ability to make Atlanta transient and his southernness mobile. Benjamin's eccentric tour uniform, however, accentuates the duo's self-definition and understanding that they are part of a larger conversation taking place. Benjamin's bold statement "Across culture, darker people suffer more. Why?" highlights his own worldly travels while articulating his awareness of the suffering of black and brown bodies across the world.

Perhaps most stunning is the statement's resuscitation of a demand for attention to the black and brown bodies that suffer across the South, a return to the civil rights rhetoric of the 1950s and 1960s. Francesca Royster's description of post-soul eccentric figures in her book *Sounding Like a No-No: Queer Sounds and Eccentric Acts in the Post-Soul Era* applies to Benjamin's theatrics as eccentric figures' "outsized performance of their own personae and selves, as well as invented characters, is a significant aspect of their eccentricity or strangeness, and provides a space for lampooning and critiquing post and present versions of blackness."[19] Benjamin's use of style reckons with the evolution of his identities over the course of his career. His performance of past tracks simultaneously coexists with his present perspective on his (southern) blackness. André Benjamin uses fashion to "navig[ate] a set of reference points that include the past as well as the future."[20] His use of his body and clothing purports his agency from the past and present. For both Benjamin and Patton, fashion serves as a site of mobility not only for their personal definitions of southernness but also for their position within a larger construction of southernness.

Aside from performing their catalog, the staging for each performance speaks further to their navigation of time and space. Their sensitivity to temporality and space takes center stage in the form of a prominent see-through black box onstage. The large box, four large screens for visual effects, represents multiple definitions of a black box: the black box as an epicenter of memory, the southern slang for a woman's vagina ("hot box"), and a tangible representation of their pushback against being "boxed into" scripts of race and gender as seen in society at large and in hip-hop. Further, the minimal use of props—with the exception of a replica of Patton's Aunt Renee's kitchen table and a Headland and Delowe street sign—suggests OutKast's mastery of time while sustaining a grasp of the current moment. The black box onstage makes OutKast's personal and cultural memories physically tangible. The memories-as-markers of OutKast's trajectory to superstardom are kept in the black box: their struggle to find their voices and retain a connection to their roots (like Aunt Renee's kitchen table) are protected and showcased onstage using this box.

Because OutKast consistently and calculatedly performed a contemporary southern black hip-hop identity, their music serves as a blueprint for other southern black creators to examine their experiences and speak their truth to power. As Benjamin stated in his acceptance speech over two decades earlier, they were the demo nobody wanted to hear, a demographic overlooked and underappreciated as creators. OutKast's ability to transform rejection into inspiration as then unsung creators offers insight into how hip-hop southerners view themselves and their experiences. OutKast provides a map for viewing the contemporary roots of southernness: a cultural and conceptual undertaking that is necessary to make room for newer articulations of southern blackness outside of the gaze of nonsoutherners who do not possess the sensibilities necessary to see the black South for the complex sociocultural landscape it is. Although OutKast is now well-received and celebrated, their initial effort to construct a southern hip-hop landscape is a useful intervention for creating an alternative contemporary southern black consciousness.

TWO: SPELLING OUT THE WORK

I finished Kiese Laymon's 2013 debut novel *Long Division* curled up in my grandfather's favorite recliner. Paw Paw loved the brown leather chair because it was directly in front of the television and adjacent to the stovepipe fireplace. The worn leather in the bottom of the seat, stretched thin from years of use but forgiving against my weight, let me sink in deeply and held me tight, a last hug from Paw Paw, who had died four years earlier. Although both my grandparents were elementary and middle school educators, it was my Paw Paw who nurtured my love of reading. Reading *Long Division* conjured memories of learning to read in Paw Paw's chair, propped on his lap while sounding out two or three words per thick and easily grabbable page in beginner books borrowed from our library. Fairy tales, talking animals, fantasy, and Norman Bridwell's *Clifford the Big Red Dog* books were my favorites. Seeking myself in the stories I devoured—young, spirited southern black girls with lopsided ponytails and ribbons like Cassie Logan in Mildred Taylor's *Roll of Thunder Hear My Cry* series—was especially rewarding. No matter what world I visited or tried to build in my mind, Paw Paw's chair was always the foundation.

It was my primary site of literacy that bolstered the significance of storytelling. Paw Paw's stories of growing up in Jim Crow Athens, Georgia, blended with my own coming-of-age in post–civil rights Albany. Storytelling was an important means of sharing, creating, and spreading knowledge across generational, cultural, and historical boundaries. As I graduated from Little Golden Books to chapter books and textbooks—my grandmother Nana Boo was always at the helm, supplying my demands for new and challenging reading material—Paw Paw remained central to my voracious reading appetite by offering to serve as a sounding board for what I was reading and its application to my views of the world. And, with a curt smile and gruff nod of his head, Paw Paw reinforced my voracious reading by speaking his truth over my love of stories: "That's good. Real good, Gina Lou," he would say after listening to my ramblings. "Gina Lou" was Paw Paw's nickname for me when I was being feisty or adamant. "It's good that you love to read. Just remember, now: reading is a powerful thing. They tried to keep books from us. What white people didn't want black people to know was put into books. Still is."

I was always fascinated by Paw Paw's depiction of books as tangible evidence of secret white knowledge and its intentional hiding from black people. White people's sensibilities surrounding the social, cultural, and historical anxieties of black folks reading in the South remains rooted in a narrative that southern black life is anti-intellectual and that black southerners who read are extraordinary. If one were to map out the literary archaeology of southern black life, a dominant focus of southern black writers is a peculiar stoicism that is heralded as exceptional rather than the norm.[1] The underlying emotional current of that stoicism as a response to the daily trauma and tensions of living in the South is amplified by nonsoutherners. Trauma remains an overriding marker of southern black culture, especially its literature. Yet, in his writing, although Laymon is aware of this literary heritage, he traverses southern black sociocultural trauma to create a form of storytelling that complicates trauma, past pain, and white supremacy as vulnerability. Perhaps most important about Laymon's storytelling is his embrace of messy southern black narratives, the inclusion of respectable and disrespectable black bodies and narratives that reflect the complexity of the contemporary southern black sociocultural landscape. This is especially significant when thinking about Laymon's place in Mississippi's literary heritage, as black trauma is a permanent export from the state. The state is steeped in terrifying racial history and swirls throughout its contemporary literary exports, including the works of the poet Natasha Trethewey and the writers Jesmyn Ward, Angie Thomas, and Laymon.[2] Yet other contemporary writers have drawn on Mississippi's history of racial terror to speak to the racial terrors of the present. Consider Paul Beatty's 1996 novel *The White Boy Shuffle*. In the opening pages, the protagonist Gunnar Kaufman shares his family tree with the reader. His father, Rölf Kaufman, grew up in Yeehaw, Mississippi. On the night of his graduation, Rölf participates in a hazing ritual that Beatty satirizes as "assimilation":

My father fondly recalled the laughs and cold celebratory summer vacation Dixie beers he shared with the good ol' boy senior class after their macabre reenactment of the Schwerner, Goodman, and Chaney murders. Rölf played Chaney, two Down syndrome kids from special-ed class reprised the roles of the hapless miscreant Jews, and three carloads of football players acted as the vigilante sheriffs. . . . After a few miles of horn-blaring, bumper-to-bumper tailgating and beer cans sounding off the windows like tin hailstones, Yeehaw's phony finest grew bored and forced my father's car to a stop. My father smiled weakly as the starting quarterback, Plessy "Go Deep" Ferguson, purposefully approached the driver's side. The strong-armed wishbone navigator par excellence opened the door with his scholarship hands and asked my father, "What are you SNCCering about? Get it, fellas? SNCC—snickering?"[3] The rest of the team burst out in laughter and proceeded to pull the scared "student activists" out of the car, taking turns cuffing my dad and the retarded kids about the face, swinging them by the ankles into the muddy bog that ran alongside the highway. Later that night all the players in the living theater met in the glade behind the courthouse for a few wrap-party beers. A campfire's glowing flames lit up a keg placed next to a thick-trunked Southern pine known as a swing-low tree. Shadows of the strong-limbed branches flickered across soused contemplative faces. My father drank so much he passed out. He came to naked, his entire body spray-painted white, his face drool-glued against the trunk of the swing-low tree. He ran home under the sinking Mississippi moon, his white skin tingling with assimilation.

Heavily exaggerated and full of wince-inducing moments before this re-counting of Rölf's background, Beatty conjures up Mississippi's violent history in the form of the lynchings of the Freedom Riders Michael Schwerner, Andrew Goodman, and James Chaney—perhaps the most infamous incident of racial violence in Mississippi, besides the death of Emmett Till. Beatty uses Rölf's involvement in reenacting their deaths as an entry point for interrogating Rölf's cowardice as a black man. Rölf's desire for acceptance by his white classmates undermines Chaney's courageous efforts for social change. Beatty roots Rölf's weakness in his southern upbringing, drawing on stereotypical and immediately recognizable tropes of southernness as backward, such as naming Rölf's hometown Yeehaw or naming the star quarterback Plessy Ferguson, a pun on the 1896 Supreme Court case that mandated the legality of "separate but equal" and the open embrace of segregation in the Deep South. It is important to note that the senior class's parody of the Freedom Riders' murders takes place in the immediate aftermath of *Brown v. Board of Topeka*, the Supreme Court case that reversed *Plessy v. Ferguson* and declared segregation unconstitutional. Thus, Plessy Ferguson's abuse of Rölf and their disabled classmates signifies upon white southerners' denouncement of the court ruling and their refusal to integrate. Beatty intentionally muddies the intersections of integration and assimilation, forcing them to overlap in awkward and exaggerated ways to speak to Rölf's personal history.

Furthermore, and perhaps most terrifying, the tension increases as the figurative and performative violence shifts to the pursuit of actual violence. The increasingly drunk participants in the reenactment—on all sides—begin to consider becoming an actual lynch mob: "Shadows of the strong-limbed branches flickered across soused contemplative faces." Their drunkenness, paired with the eerie campfire glow over "swing-low" or lynching tree, blurs the past and present. Rölf, still eager to be accepted by the drunk pseudo-mob's standards, plays along by getting drunk himself, an act that suggests his intentional numbing of the increasingly dangerous situation. He passes out drunk but finds himself still connected to the tree, a haunting reminder of those who may have been lynched at the same tree in the past. Rölf runs home, naked and spray-painted white, a jab at his attempt to integrate or be white, "his white skin tingling with assimilation."[4] The tingle of assimilation can be read as a sensory response to the trauma Rölf faced *and* avoided by interacting with his white classmates. Beatty satirizes Rölf's "physical" transition to an oreo, slang for black people acting white, as a coming-of-age moment for Rölf, who grew up on the cusp of the post–civil rights South. Rölf's coming-of-age falls within Mississippi's, as an overt symbol of the peculiarity of white supremacy is signified in the white boys' nonchalant treatment of black death as an entertaining spectacle.[5]

While Beatty's satire briefly uses Mississippi as a microcosm of the peculiarity of white supremacy in the post–civil rights era, the author's rendering of Mississippi also points to an underlying regional bias against the American South. It is more useful for nonsoutherners to leave the sociohistorical complexities of southern black people's fight for integration—in this instance heavily exaggerated, ahistorical, and flat—as a crutch for working through the peculiarities of race and agency in contemporary American society. Southern writers like Laymon are sensitive to this juxtaposition, and they create narratives that simultaneously present southernness as an apex of American identity while making space to question how the South reflects the challenges of race in the present. And, like other contemporary black writers, Laymon uses hip-hop as the foundation for creating literary spaces as sites of witnessing the stories and experiences that exist between-the-cracks of the civil rights movement. Hip-hop allows post–civil rights writers like Laymon to create literary spaces where the past is in conversation with the present and future. This is especially prevalent in *Long Division* where Laymon uses time travel in rural Mississippi via a hole in the ground, a symbolic image of his reckoning with the past, present, and future of southern black Mississippians. The foundation of Laymon's maneuvering between multiple sets of southern black experiences is hip-hop culture.

With southern hip-hop, Laymon literally writes himself into existence. For example, in the prologue of his 2013 collection of essays *How to Slowly Kill Yourself and Others in America*, he states it is important to read his collection like an album, his essays serving as "tracks" or "as songs with multiple voices and layered musicality."[6] Laymon also uses ad libs and pauses reminiscent of rappers, who try to push their narratives farther while pacing themselves to stay on track. Consider his discussion of hip-hop and localism in "Hip-Hop Stole My Southern Black Boy." In this essay, Laymon expounds on the multiple ways in which hip-hop simultaneously buffers and registers his contemporary southernness and masculinity. He starts with a memory of conducting a freestyle rap cipher in the boys' bathroom of his middle school in Jackson. Led by B. Dazzle, the younger brother of the pioneering Mississippi rapper Brad "Kamikaze" Franklin, Laymon recalls "slouch[ing] between two urinals, hands cupped over mouth, providing a weak beat box while B. Dazzle went on and on and on."[7] B. Dazzle's presence emphasized not only a heterosexual and urban black masculine cool pose for rural southerners but also their ability to embrace and re-create hip-hop culture as a sophisticated art form. Aside from B. Dazzle's familiarity with hip-hop because of his older brother's emceeing, B. Dazzle embodied Laymon's grappling with how to localize and respect hip-hop aesthetics. Those aesthetics were rooted in one's locality and distance from New York. In Laymon's description of the bathroom stall, it physically and culturally embodies the concept of the "Dirty South": "dirty" young black boys crouched between bathroom stalls while black and living in the state of Mississippi. It is important to note that Laymon recalls his first cipher in 1992, at a moment when hip-hop is still considered solely a New York affair. B. Dazzle and his brother Kamikaze, rumored to have kinfolk who lived in the South Bronx—hip-hop's origin site—added to the splendor of Laymon's perception of B. Dazzle's embodiment of hip-hop. B. Dazzle's emphasis on calling their bathroom rhymes a "cipher" instead of a "rap circle" also signifies upon the underlying anxieties of southernness as a localized account of unsophisticated blackness. The uphill battle of being "artistically inferior and local" or "the ashy black-hand side" of hip-hop paralleled black southerners' struggle against being the ignored side of the contemporary black experience. B. Dazzle's emphasis on being "hip-hop" instead of "rap" speaks to the yearning of many early southern hip-hop aficionados who wanted to be recognized as hip-hop.[8] In its earliest manifestations in Laymon's life, the cipher was more than a space for boasting or "confessing themselves into the world over a beat box."[9] The cipher was an act of imposed witnessing, or a belief about what hip-hop *should be* for him instead of its actual significance.

The disconnect between hip-hop's New York–centric focus and Laymon's position as a black boy from Mississippi initially haunts him. He writes: "Back then, fifteen minutes into our lunch period, seven of us descended into what we called the B-Boy bathroom. B-Boy for us meant neither Breaker Boy, Bad Boy, or Bronx Boy; it meant Black Boy."[10] Laymon's description of his bathroom cipher with seven friends suggests that New York was not the genesis of his hip-hop, much to the chagrin of B. Dazzle. Laymon recognizes that his boyhood and country-ness are disconnected from hip-hop's New York–centric labels and expressivity: "Breaker Boy," a signifier of break dance; "Bad Boy," a signifier of Bad Boy records, an immediately recognizable producer and image of New York hip-hop; and the Bronx, hip-hop's birthplace, do not register in the South with the same resonance as New York hip-hoppers.

Rather, Laymon's genesis point for hip-hop was localized to Mississippi, and bounced off of other accounts of Mississippi black boys who shared the same local space with him. Further, Laymon's point of departure for positioning himself in hip-hop is as a "Black Boy," a reference to Richard Wright's autobiography *Black Boy*.[11] Hip-hop serves an entry point for Laymon to think through his life experiences as a country black boy living in the post–civil rights era. He writes, "We wanted to use hip-hop's brash boast, confessional, and critique to unapologetically order the chaos of our country lives through country lenses, with little regard for whether or not it sounded like *real* hip-hop. We were on our way to realizing that we were blues people, familiar in some way or another with dirt . . . and we liked it that way."[12] For Laymon, hip-hop's usefulness lay in its ability to speak to how the South ebbed and flowed on its own terms.

In particular, Laymon pays attention to the generational tensions of black exceptionalism and the expectations imposed on younger southern blacks. He writes: "The seven of us had similar dreams of being divine emcees, too, though we knew geography wouldn't allow it. Plus, our mamas and grandparents had other plans, and they made sure we became multiple dreamers who actualized boring dreams like becoming managers, counterfeiters, computer engineers, racketeers, sergeants, pimps, and college professors."[13] Dreaming of becoming an emcee—a marker of contemporary southern black dreaming—was a stepping-stone rather than the final destination in meeting the expectations of older black folks, who were unfamiliar with or refused to acknowledge hip-hop as a "respectable" profession or culture. Laymon's conceptualization of "dreaming" here is a major signifier of the tensions that exist from older southern black generations' expectations of younger southern black folks to be exceptional. There is an explicit expectation that young southern blacks "make good" of themselves because the way has been paved by previous struggles and social movements. Young southern black folks' success should follow the blueprint of respectable visibility and paths outlined by previous generations. Laymon points out, however, that there is no cookie-cutter avenue to being successful in the South and that it is often tinged with unrespectable means. Young black southerners' ability to be "multiple dreamers" means being cognizant of the type of racial and socioeconomic equality Dr. King referenced in his "I Have a Dream" speech, and at the same time carving out space to create their own agency. In other words, Laymon points out that "all them dreams ain't respectable," sprinkling in the hoped for and lived outcomes of King's generation of dreamers. The seven occupations Laymon references in this statement—arguably the achievements of Laymon's group of friends from the bathroom cipher—is particularly strong because of the mixed bag of outcomes and folks. The intentional placement of counterfeiters, racketeers, and pimps between "boring" but respectable jobs of management, military service, and teaching signifies the blending of past and present forms of southern black respectability, exceptionalism, and success. Laymon situates himself in the belief that hip-hop is the newest layer of being dirt folk, southerners aware that their creativity and existence might be marginalized but never undermined because of its introspective focus and roots in the local: "I now accept the Black Boys, Invisible Men, Native Sons, and Blues People who grandfolked hip-hop into existence."[14] Laymon's foundational understanding of hip-hop in the South later helped him update and position himself within a larger lineage of southern black cultural expression.

In particular, I am interested in how Laymon uses the music of the southern hip-hop duo OutKast to frame his navigation of contemporary southern blackness in his novel *Long Division*. Both Laymon and Out-Kast signify upon the dirtiness of the contemporary black experience to create distinctive tropes in storytelling that speak to the blurred binaries of southernness, blackness, and communal agency. For example, in "Hip-Hop Stole My Southern Black Boy," Laymon indicates an early cognizance of his marginalization within hip-hop: "From our position, the black girls in the hall were positioned in the same way we were positioned as Southern eavesdroppers of New York hip-hop. . . . Some would get close as they could to the crack of the door, but they could never come all the way in."[15] In this instance Laymon recognizes both his position as a hip-hop outcast and the girls listening to their cipher in the hallway. He demonstrates a working awareness of difference in southern and northern blackness via hip-hop aesthetics. Laymon's rendering of cipher in this instance alludes to the collective action of his folk, fellow (local) southern black boys who also enjoyed and attempted to assert themselves within hip-hop. Laymon and his friends' bathroom cipher created space that ran parallel to a northeastern hip-hop aesthetic.

Here I would like to make the connection between Laymon and Out-Kast in their use of marginalization to establish contemporary southern black agency in hip-hop. Like OutKast, Laymon's most significant underlying theme in *Long Division* is his attempt to define the process of achieving freedoms in the post–civil rights black South. Laymon's characters and plot grapple with how to establish a new precedent for southern black folks' freedom in a contemporary cultural landscape. Laymon presents this process as "stank," yet another nod to OutKast and their rendering of Stankonia as "the place from which all funky things come,"[16] a messy gray space of discomfort and less-than-respectable elements of "getting free." The literal and conceptual funk of southern black folks and their agency parallels similar tropes of the black South as a freedom space in OutKast's body of work.

Specifically, I assert that Laymon's use of OutKast and their album *Aquemini* as an inspiration for developing *Long Division*'s storyline provides a conceptual framework for thinking through and presenting southern hip-hop as a conceptual framework in turn for contemporary southern black storytelling. *Long Division*'s epigraph quotes lines from an André Benjamin verse in the song "Aquemini": "Twice upon a time there was a *boy* who died / and lived happily ever after / but that's another chapter."[17] The verse signifies upon Benjamin's astrological sign of Gemini or "the twins" and addresses the possibility not only of a split personality but also of split realities for the same boy, which could have differing outcomes. *Long Division* picks up this theme, when Laymon introduces two protagonists named City who live parallel lives in different time periods connected via a book also titled *Long Division*. City, whose real name Citoyen is French for citizen, exists in the years 2013 and 1985. Differences in font styles alert the reader to the two different perspectives of the characters named City. The 1985 City time travels between the years 1985, 1964, and 2013, representing three historical moments in southern black history. Yet both characters live in the post–civil rights eras: 1985 City lives closer to the ushering in of the post–civil rights South and 2013 City lives in the well-established and now multiple-generations' populated post–civil rights era. In 1964 the Mississippi Freedom Summer project took place, a collective effort of civil rights organizations spearheaded by the Student Nonviolent Coordinating Committee to help register blacks to vote and assist with literacy. The Mississippi Freedom Democratic Party was also founded by Fannie Lou Hamer, Ella Baker, and Robert Parris Moses. The year 1985 is a personal historical moment for Laymon. He shares in an interview that 1985 is important because "it's the year that *Fat Boys Are Back* comes out. [It is] also a year that *Price Is Right, Young and the Restless*, and [Michael] Jordan are important. Most importantly, we [southerners] need to be in the midst of Reagonomics."[18] The year 2013, the contemporary setting of the novel, signifies upon the South after Hurricane Katrina and in the immediate aftermath of the death of Trayvon Martin and the trial surrounding his murder. Laymon's use of Martin's death as a historical signifier of southern blackness is important because it resituates his death within southern sensibilities that also helped previous generations work through similar deaths of young black men like Emmett Till.

Further, 2013 City's post–civil rights South is rooted in the aftermath of Hurricane Katrina, a sociocultural and physical reworking of the southern landscape. The ending of the first bar establishes an early premise that the novel will not wrap up easily, comfortably, or to the liking of Laymon or his audience. There is always another unspoken or unfinished chapter in southern black storytelling, a looming signifier that fuels Laymon's plot. Further, the use of Benjamin's verse here establishes OutKast as Laymon's point of departure without losing sight of the black South in its past, present, or future storm. For example, Laymon's imagining of Melahatchie, Mississippi, the fictitious coastal town where the bulk of *Long Division* action takes place, could be read as an extension of OutKast's Stankonia rather than an evocation of William Faulkner's imaginary Mississippi county of Yoknapatawpha. Faulkner, like most southern white writers, featured black characters within the context of a white (male) gaze but never as the center of their own existence. Rather, I argue that Melahatchie and its black characters are squarely situated within a black folks' gaze that does not center southern whiteness as its foundation. Instead of being an aside to a white southern lineage, Laymon uses hip-hop to establish a separate branch of contemporary southern black storytelling.

Laymon's use of two protagonists intentionally centers young black southerners on a line straddling past and present, with their expectations of futurity lodged between their acts of imagining and the historical signposts of trauma and resistance common to southern black life and culture. From this perspective, Laymon's interrogation of young southern black duality is situated in southern hip-hop and thus calculatedly messy and human, offering insight into the daily challenges and triumphs of being southern and black in a contemporary setting.

Consider Laymon's characterization of 2013 City and his classmate LaVander Peeler as they prepare to compete in the "Can You Use That Word in a Sentence?" competition, a southern equivalent to the Scripps National Spelling Bee. As a result of southerners feeling "geographically biased," the competition focused on the mastery of sentence completion and offered the prize of a $75,000 scholarship. The "Can You Use That Word in a Sentence?" competition is a pun on the phonetic and socially stigmatic awkwardness—stank—surrounding the ways that southerners speak and interact with themselves and nonsoutherners. Like Laymon and his friends in the middle school bathroom in 1992, City and Lavelle freestyle and rap among their classmates in the form of elaborate and sometimes just ridiculously long sentences. For example, LaVander Peeler expounds on African Americans while dissing City: "African-Americans are generally a lot more ignorant than white Americans, and if you're an African-American boy and you beat not only African-American girls but white American boys and white American girls, who are, all things considered, less ignorant than you by nature— in something like making sentences, in a white American state like Mississippi—you are, all things considered, a special African-American boy destined for riches, unless you're a homeless white fat homosexual African-American boy with mommy issues who I shall beat like a knock-kneed slave tonight at the nationals."[19] LaVander's focus black exceptionalism as a means of success reflects an implicit expectation for young southern blacks to move forward because the way is paved or the mountaintop is flat. What is overlooked—and what LaVander realizes later during the "Can You Use That Word in a Sentence Competition"—is that talent and hard work only get black folks so far. LaVander's "calling out" of City as a "white fat homosexual African-American boy" is not only a nod to the dozens but also an understanding of whiteness and homosexuality as the ultimate diss, especially in the South. City doesn't understand LaVander's reasoning and says "he's always praising white people in his sentences, but then he'll turn around and call me 'white' in the same sentence like it's a diss."[20]

City's Ellisonian moment onstage, a jarring realization of his black blossoming masculinity, runs parallel to Ralph Ellison's anonymous black male characters in *Invisible Man* and "King of the Bingo Game."[21] City is given the word "niggardly." He says, "I kept squinting, trying to see out beyond the lights, beyond the stage."[22] City attempts to see beyond this particular moment—another slight nod toward the novel's focus on trying to imagine one's self in the future—but also a parallel to Ellison's King of the Bingo Game. After winning a chance at the bingo board for much needed money, the King of the Bingo Game—also a southerner—stumbles onstage but is hit by "a light so sharp and bright that for a moment it blinded him."[23] Performing exceptionalism is underwritten as a sure bet—literally in "King of the Bingo Game"—for achieving success. But I am most drawn toward the overlap between King of the Bingo Game's refusal to let go of the wheel button and City's fixation on his brush and the competition buzzer to alert City to take a seat. King of the Bingo Game is beaten by police but the button is central to his construction of power. He believes holding it places him in control of himself and the situation. City's brush is his center of power. As he becomes increasingly anxious, he fumbles with the brush and strokes his hair. The buzzer, however, is a sonic marker of City's increasing self-consciousness and the realization that he and LaVander are not taken seriously as competitors. Each time City becomes "woke" or speaks a truth that is politically incorrect or uncomfortable, the buzzer goes off. After the final buzzer—and the judges' realization that City is a teenager and not Pavlov's dog—City yells, "And fuck white folks! I yelled at the light and, for the first time all night, thought about whether my grandma was watching. 'My name is City, and if you don't know, now you know, nigga!'"[24] The seamless blending of Notorious B.I.G.'s ending line on each verse of "Juicy" and City's concern about whether or not his grandmother was watching and ultimately the fear of embarrassing her demonstrates the continuous challenge of balancing one's self-agency and anger with the expectations of your folks: "What you gone have me looking like out here doing that?" or "It ain't just about you."

"Da Art of Storytellin'": OutKast's *Aquemini*

As established in chapter 1, OutKast's third album *Aquemini* is a memoiresque navigation of their increasingly experimental and fluid reckoning with southern blackness. *Aquemini* is both an exercise and exorcism of the dangers of nostalgia, a tangible fear for the two rappers in their quest to continue to evolve and create new music and articulations of southern black identities. To grapple with the messy intersections of southern blackness as acts of imagination and temporality, OutKast fine-tunes their act of storytelling. From this perspective, storytelling is a theorization of how to move forward without losing sight of the past, a blend of oral tradition and performance of the sociohistorical lineage of a contemporary southern black culturescape. For example, *Aquemini* features a thread of skits serving as transitions between songs and as markers that challenge the listener to follow the shifts in perspectives that OutKast presents in their stories. OutKast's use of skits on their albums are experimental, providing alternative realities and grappling with the duo's view of themselves and how they present themselves to others.

The use of skits on the *Aquemini* album in particular indicates how the group tries to avoid the tethering of their previous work to the constantly changing tide of their work and view of themselves in the world. For example, the first skit on the album comes after the track "Return of the G" and takes place in a record store. The manager helps two male customers with music, joking about their choice in music from reggae to the latest hip-hop music. The manager then tries to sell the two customers the latest OutKast album and the men refuse. "First they was some pimps, man," one of the men criticizes, "then they was aliens, or some genies, or some shit."[25] Because of his inability to place OutKast in one category, he dismisses them entirely: "I ain't fuckin' with them no more, man."[26] The skit is the group parodying themselves and their street credibility, especially André Benjamin, who was starting to experiment not only lyrically but sartorially, separating himself from the expected performance of hip-hop masculinity. Benjamin explains the skit as "a parody of everything going on at the time. Back then all the hood record labels were called stuff like Slap a Bitch records or Big Dick Records so we made up the name Pimp Trick Gangsta Clique."[27] While the skit's focus is OutKast's awareness that their legitimacy is being challenged because they run multiple lanes of identity, it is also a space of hypothetical situations. Benjamin discloses the kernel of truth present in the fictitious group: that he and the Dungeon Family members Sleepy Brown and Cee-Lo Green actually recorded under the name but never released music.

Further, the record store skit on the album offered an alternative reality that came true in some regard: the rise of technological music services, such as streaming, wiped out the record store culture, which makes the skit both humorous and playful. Record stores went beyond selling music to serving as communal spaces: artists visiting stores to sign albums and meet fans or simply people gathering to share and learn about new releases in a brick-and-mortar setting are things of the past. Our dependency on technology, which OutKast warns us about on the track "Synthesizer" later on the album, wipes out the record culture in which many debated OutKast's work and impact.

Still, most of the storytelling that stands out happens in the music. For the purposes of this chapter, I am especially interested in the couplet of songs "Da Art of Storytellin'." The theme of duality spans both songs: the voices of André Benjamin and Big Boi, the duality of the consequences both men face for their actions, and the duality of the beginning of the world (i.e., the blossoming of their sexual prowess) and its ending (the literal end of the world as they know it). OutKast's focus on coming-of-age and loss of innocence are useful tools for contextualizing Laymon's novel *Long Division* as a reckoning with not only hip-hop as a reflection of black youth but also the long-standing and painful work of situating their youth within a landscape of historical and social terror for black people living in the American South. Using "Da Art of Storytellin'," parts 1 and 2 provides bookends to Laymon's use of speculative fiction to wander through and interrogate the duality of stories being told in *Long Division*.

Country Black Girl Existentialism

Reading OutKast's theorization of storytelling as a duality of temporality and performance provides a working model for how to engage the multiplicities of southern black experience. Of particular interest is how black women and girls fit into the multiplicities of southern black experiences. This is especially evident in hip-hop, where the bodies and lives of black women and girls often run adjacent to but not in immediate conversation with southern black men and boys. This in turn reflects a need for space where southern black women and girls can center themselves and speak their truth to power. Southern black women and respectability are inextricably linked, even in the present. The ideology of southern black women's respectability politics remains deeply connected to the historian Evelyn Brooks Higginbotham's initial theorization of this ideology as an extension of presence in the black church.[28] Another name for southern black women's politics of respectability is a politics of being ladylike and proper, a fault line that extends beyond the walls of the black church into a lasting monument of womanhood for southern black communities. This body of politics remains suffocatingly connected to the visibility and ultimate humanity of black women in the South. I am not immune to it: my grandmother very much subscribes to being a lady. I've been asked and often wonder about what makes southern black girls special, and I have yet to be able to explain my inherited country black girl magic to nonrural black folks. Robin Boylorn's autoethnographic study of rural southern black women in her family and in Sweetwater, North Carolina, in *Sweetwater: Black Women Narratives and Narratives of Resistance*, offered wording for thinking through how southern black women navigate between the inextricable linkage of racial and sexist marginalization in the South. Boylorn describes the linking of her collegiate training to her background as "community intelligence." "Community intelligence" for southern black women is often nonverbal or highly localized to reflect their experiences. This type of southern home-training is often generational, resembling an heirloom passed down over the years—there are words to live by that only southern black women would embrace and understand. However, I suggest that threads of familiarity, or what Boylorn suggests are "moments of recognition and resonance," create a network of southern black women trying to talk each other through southern life.[29]

For contemporary southern black girls and ultimately for women like me, southern black girlhood is unique in that it is a navigation of how to "carry myself" as a lady—often the crux of any type of respectability for black women—while situating myself in a sociocultural moment where being ladylike or quiet or politically correct does not mean everything will be all right. From this perspective, I am struck by both Laymon's and OutKast's rendering of contemporary southern black girlhood. Their offerings of flawed but memorable girl characters like Sasha Thumper and Shalaya Crump suggest a realization of southern black girlhood as a lens for looking through their maleness but also establish a sense of agency that pushes back against southernness as black and masculine. Both OutKast and Laymon dabble in what I would theorize as country black girl existentialism, by which southern black women and girls actively search and work toward asserting themselves into a culture and space that would rather render them invisible and attach them to a collective southern black maleness instead of to their own voice. Those conversations between black women and girls are nonlinear, crossing across time and space like the southern culturescapes that fostered them. For example, in her book *A Voice from the South*, first published in 1892, Anna Julia Cooper calls for an extra consideration of southern black women and girls by black men, classifying us as "that large, bright, promising fatally beautiful class that stand shivering like a delicate plantlet before the fury of tempestuous elements, so full of possibilities, yet so sure of destruction."[30] I'm struck by the metaphor of southern black women "shivering like a delicate plantlet." Cooper presents southern black womanhood as vulnerable, even dainty, when she includes "delicate" and "shivering" as descriptors. This is a far cry from the hardened reality many southern black women faced as laborers. As a formerly enslaved woman, Cooper knew firsthand about black women's inability to claim autonomy over themselves and their work. From this perspective, her writing of herself and other black women into vulnerability is a powerful act of interior and posterior world-building, a place where southern black women's voices are noted and noteworthy.[31] Cooper's description of southern black women and girls as a "fatally beautiful class" is both a call of love and a recognition of trauma: she recognizes that black women and girls lack agency and influence not only in the African American community but in American society at large, and she calls for protection and ultimately the witnessing of their humanity. Cooper's call for southern black women pairs their thingness—their domestic and social capital—with hopes of care for them as delicate "things" worthy of this care and attention so as to thrive. Still, it is not lost on Cooper that her call for the care and attention of southern black women and girls is a plea that may go unanswered—the fatal end of black women and girls at the hands of themselves and their communities is still a very tangible reality.

Another voice from the South in conversation with Cooper is Zora Neale Hurston, a champion for recognizing the complicated nature of southern black womanhood. Hurston, a southern black woman from Eatonville, Florida, used multiple mediums to capture and archive the experiences southern black communities dominantly from the perspective of southern black women. Hurston's intentional use of southern black dialect was criticized by many of her public and academic contemporaries and literary peers, who wished to use black artistry as a springboard for demonstrating black people's ability to be as sophisticated and recognizable as their white counterparts. Underappreciated, however, was Hurston's sophisticated use of dialect as an act of reckoning: her attention to the language used in the oral traditions of southern story-telling and the use of those stories as the literal mapping out of the thoughts and experiences of southern black women. Hurston's use of dialect is a literary homage to the significance of sound and southern black life: the dialect she recorded and transcribed acknowledges the multiplicities of southern black spaces and their inhabitants. In her well-known 1937 novel *Their Eyes Were Watching God*, Janie Crawford, a fortyish Floridian black woman, returns to her hometown of Eatonville after the death of her husband, Tea Cake. Wearing overalls and her hair loosely down her back—two countersartorial choices for being black and ladylike in public—Janie arrives back home at dusk, an ominous symbol of her widowhood and the death of her respectability via the gossip of the "ladies" in Eatonville. Hurston uses dialect as a vehicle for speculative storytelling in the form of a prodigal narrative for southern black women. With no frills and no desire to sound proper or sophisticated, Janie tells her story to her best friend Pheoby.[32] Hurston's characterization of Janie as speaking for herself and centering her truth as power while those around her would rather situate her in the narratives and experiences of her ex-husbands.

Like Janie and other black women characters in the southern literary canon such as Celie and Shug Avery from Alice Walker's novel *The Color Purple*, I suggest that contemporary southern black writers like Laymon and Jesmyn Ward through her characters Esch and Leonie from *Salvage the Bones: A Novel* (2011) and *Sing, Unburied, Sing: A Novel* (2017) exist in the same sociocultural combine of country black girl existentialism. Whereas writers like Cooper, Hurston, and Walker offer perspectives of southern black women in the early and mid-twentieth century, Laymon and Ward offer an entry points for considering how southern hip-hop interweaves with country black existentialism for black women and girls in the present. However, for the sake of this chapter I focus on the communal bond between Laymon's Shalaya Crump and OutKast's character Sasha Thumper from their song "Da Art of Storytellin' (Part 1)." These characters are communal in the sense that they provide a call-and-response over time and space that puts their desires and vulnerability at the center of contemporary southern blackness in tandem with their male counterparts. Not only do Sasha Thumper and Shalaya Crump remind me of girls I grew up with in southwest Georgia—a memory that situates me within the community intelligence and cipher taking place between both characters—but they are speaking their truths to power using the experiences and language available to them in their respective local areas.

In "Da Art of Storytellin' (Part 1)," OutKast introduces two black girls, Suzy Screw and Sasha Thumper. Big Boi weaves a story of Suzy Screw as sexually available and desirable yet cheap, demanding little from him in exchange for his brief affections. Suzy Screw puns on the hip-hop colloquialism "to screw" or have sexual intercourse. Although dominated (and aware that she is dominated) by a male gaze, Suzy Screw does not exist in a vacuum. She "had a partner" named Sasha Thumper, a more cerebral and "self-actualized" character who is far more than a riff of Benjamin's imagination.

Sasha Thumper is memorable for Benjamin because, as he declares, "I remember her number like the summer." There is little sexual tension in Benjamin's conjuring of Sasha Thumper's character. Rather, Sasha Thumper is a much more painful reminder of the difficulty of life not only for southern black children but southern black girls. When Benjamin asks Sasha about her future, her one word answer "alive" is a heartbreaking sign of her willing herself into the future. The act of living is itself a form of resistance to whatever socioeconomic or cultural circumstances affect Sasha beyond her current moment of girlhood with André Benjamin. Yet Benjamin is unable to comprehend her short remark and declaration, but makes a declaration of his own "I thought for a second and looked into her eyes / I coulda died."[33] In addition to Benjamin's acknowledging his inability to understand Sasha's position about wanting to be alive, his response is also a double entendre of death: he is foreshadowing Sasha's own demise and in falling for her, trying to love her back to life. Still, Sasha is unable to make it past the difficulties of life's hard realities: falling victim to domestic abuse, drug addiction, and ultimately dying of a drug overdose behind a school— the cultural epitome of childhood—while seven months pregnant. She was walking among the living but her will to be, to exist, was no longer part of her.

Sasha Thumper's hope to live can be found in Shalaya Crump's ellipsis.

Shalaya Crump is a working-class black girl who lives in 1985 Melahatchie, Mississippi. We are first introduced to Shalaya as exceptional because City says she is here simultaneously in the present and future. "If any other girl in 1985 said, 'the future dot-dot-dot,' she would have meant 1986 or maybe 1990 at the most. But not Shalaya Crump. I knew she meant somewhere way in the future that no one other than scientists and dope fiends had ever thought of before."[34] Far more than an allusion to Shalaya's time-traveling skills, City's description of her vision is reflective of the civil rights activists' dream for younger black southerners to take their sacrifices and be successful as well as an affirmation of her Afrofuturist country black girl magic. The ellipsis is particularly useful in identifying how Shalaya literally moves through time and space to actualize her self-agency and see herself in spaces where others cannot. Sonically, Shalaya sounds out the ellipsis, saying "dot-dot-dot" as a placeholder for how she saves room for her thoughts that are part of the past and future but struggle in the present. This struggle is affirmed by her constant retort to City to "show his work," a nod to the book's title and a reminder of Shalaya's youthfulness but wisdom beyond her years (literally and figuratively). Her sonic articulation of the ellipsis reads as a rendering of uncertainty and possibility: the ellipsis is equally a placeholder and springboard of possibility for Shalaya to imagine herself as a southern black girl in places where others cannot. The ellipsis also serves as a family heirloom: when City asks Baize what type of punctuation mark she would be, she responds, "ellipsis": "that's the dot-dot-dot you were talking about . . . the ellipsis always knows something more came before it and something more is coming after it."[35] Baize's theorization of an ellipsis fits because she recognizes that she is part of a previous story—her missing mother and father—and the "something more" or possibility of a future that she represents for both City and Shalaya.

Still, I'm particularly struck by City's understanding of Shalaya's belief in (her) future as a space where only dope fiends had ever thought about. This is a small but significant nod to Sasha Thumper's inability to see past her drug addiction into a future where she makes it out well and alive. Still, Shalaya Crump's view of the future, though optimistic, is not romanticized. When Shalaya realizes she can't find herself in the year 2013, she enlists City to help find her.

In one of City's many efforts to win over Shalaya's affections, they begin talking about invisibility and the future. In a moment reminiscent of Sasha Thumper and André Benjamin, Shalaya attempts to connect with City on an existential level. "'Yeah, yeah, City!' she grabbed my forearm and looked me in the eyes . . . what happens if we disappear in the future?"[36] City, still unable to comprehend that Shalaya was trying to assert herself in the future, continues focusing on trying to get Shalaya to love him. But after bringing City with her to the future, Shalaya says, "I'm scared because, well, I think I'm dead. Can you help me?"[37] Where Sasha Thumper wants to simply be alive, Shalaya Crump wants to make sure she stays that way. Both girls face the threat of disappearing from consciousness and memory, pointing to a larger challenge confronting young black girls and women in the South today.

Da Art of Speculation

The final seventy-five pages of *Long Division* are fast-paced and dizzying: the novel ends with Laymon's characters in a whirlwind of their own thoughts that blur into the stories that they are both creating and witnessing. The 1985 City grapples with the revelation that he and Shalaya Crump drown in Hurricane Katrina. His daughter, Baize Shephard, is a missing person from 2013 City's storyline. In a truly brilliant twist of science fiction, Baize and her father cannot stay with each other, as Baize starts to die because she is not in the right historical time period. Baize describes her symptoms of being wrongfully ahistorical as allergy symptoms, a sharp critique of the thin line that southerners walk in distinguishing between nostalgia and the number-one concrete rule of time travel: a traveler cannot change the past. "Watching Shalaya Crump love Evan smashed my heart, but lying to my daughter about what was about to happen to her made every living thing in my body just quit."[38] In addition to losing his daughter, the 1985 City also loses Shalaya Crump, who decides to stay in one of her pasts with their traveling companion Evan Altshuler, a young Jewish teenager from 1964. From one perspective, Shalaya's decision to value herself above what others want from her or how the world sees her is Morrisonian in the sense that she recognizes herself and her truth as her own best thing.[39] Shalaya wanted to fight for her own existence, itself an act of liberation. City doesn't recognize Shalaya's decision as an act of survival but as an act of betrayal: he takes Shalaya's decision to stay with Evan as a sign that Shalaya is in love with Evan rather than him. The ending of Shalaya and City's relationship is a familiar coming-of-age theme—the first heartbreak—deeply rooted in the equally familiar theme of survival through trauma as a signifier of southern blackness.

Jaded and bitter after losing Baize and Shalaya, City encounters Mama Lara, his grandmother, in a community center. City sees 2013 City's answers to the exam that he takes at the beginning of the book, and the 1985 City is confused about being unable to remember when and where he took the exam. It is important to note that the year of the test is missing, a more pronounced indicator of the fluidity and nonlinear existence of southern life and culture. Mama Lara is a mysterious, oracle-like figure who irritates City because she forces him to think about the larger picture outside of his own frustration and pain. For example, with Baize's laptop in hand, Mama Lara instructs City about the power of love and remembrance: "People disappear, City . . . we live, we wonder, we love, we lie, and we disappear" and "sometimes we appear again if we're loved."[40] The balance of wisdom in the act of southern black folks' continued living is offered as unwavering advice for any obstacle facing younger people, simply stated by many southern black elders as "keep livin'." These elders include my grandparents and Laymon's grandmother, Catherine Coleman. From this perspective, Mama Lara completely embodies and signifies on the tradition of older, wise black folks as "elders," authoritative but caring figures who seem clairvoyant in their views of the world and their experiences and place in it. As an elder, Mama Lara speculates about City's future from an arc of optimism and hope that she hopes to instill in him as a tool to thrive and progress.

City's return to the hole in the ground, the source of his ability to time travel, is also a double-edged sword of reclamation and self-discovery: the hole is a physical signifier of the historical and much speculated network of the Underground Railroad and City's effort to re-love and resurrect Baize and himself the way Mama Lara had encouraged. The 1985 City, deep in the hole and reading and writing his thoughts and experiences down in the *Long Division* book senses someone else in the hole with him, unable to see them until he lights his last match. Laymon leaves the person's identity ambiguous, as City exclaims, "You?!" which is the end of 1985 City's story. The renewed promise of tomorrow—the highest of cultural capital for older generations of southern black people—is not lost on City as he shares his optimism about the freedom to dream about tomorrow because he is learning how to love. This thread of familiarity of trauma extends into the 2013 City's life as well: his grandmother murders the white man named PotBelly who assaulted City and whom she believes killed Baize not only as an act of retaliation but as a retaliation in the name of loving a black child.

The ending of *Long Division* coincides with the second installment of "Da Art of Storytellin'," which asks the listener to speculate with Out-Kast not only about Armageddon but also about what the last rhyme that both the duo and hip-hop would ever write. The signifiers for "Da Art of Storytellin' (Part 2)" are numerous and multilayered: how does hip-hop resurrect the memories and experiences of young southern black people? How is hip-hop a rectifier of death and the more metaphorical stagnancy associated with the southern markers of identities and communities for black people? Furthermore, both Patton and Benjamin situate their speculation about the end of the world in their respective performative qualities: Patton uses his verse to remember and love his family, and Benjamin thinks about the physical environment of the South—and people's treatment of it—as an indicator of not only racism and white supremacy but also the final straw of our literal trashing of the natural world around us.

Like the ending of *Long Division*, "Da Art of Storytellin' (Part 2)" is a messy benediction that disrupts the narrative of southern black stoicism as well as the act of healing as clean-cut and sterile. Both Laymon and OutKast interrogate the spaces in which the healing takes place: in "Da Art of Storytellin' (Part 2)," OutKast's respite and shelter is the original Dungeon Family recording studio, the basement of Rico Wade's mother at 1907 Lakewood Terrace in Atlanta, and the hole in City's grandmother's backyard in *Long Division*. The two spaces are connected because of the imagery of the dungeon or underground as liberatory but never quite fulfilling the full work of becoming free. This leftover work of freedom in the South, theorized by Laymon as long division, suggests the work will never be completed. In other words, Laymon and OutKast do not sanitize southern black folks' trauma. They embrace the uncertainty of it, and trouble the foundation of trauma as a cornerstone of southern black identities. In *Long Division* and in "Da Art of Storytellin'" tracks on the *Aquemini* album, the multiplicities of southern blackness exist simultaneously in the past, present, and future.

THREE: REIMAGINING SLAVERY IN THE HIP-HOP IMAGINATION

In the opening scene of WGN's television series *Underground*, a black enslaved man named Noah (played by Aldis Hodge) is seen running through the woods at night. Noah crashes through the landscape, jumping over bushes and running in erratic patterns. He is looking for something. The camera cuts away to a white man carrying a torch and egging on a pack of dogs. Noah finds an abandoned wagon with a bell but is cornered by the patroller's dogs. The dog attacks and bites Noah's leg as Noah gropes around on the ground to find something to defend himself. He hits the dog over the head and hides in the forest underbrush, ramming his nose into the crook of his elbow and shirt. The scene ends with Noah being hit upside the head by the patroller, and then cuts away to the title of the series. The opening scene of the series is dizzying and heart-pounding.

While it is visually stunning—the scene does not hold back on the multiple types of physical and psychological violence endured by runaway slaves trying to escape to the North—*Underground*'s opening is most jarring because of its use of hip-hop as an accompaniment depicting Noah's desperation. Simultaneous with Noah's first appearance onscreen is the sound of crashing cymbals and percussion from Kanye West's song "Black Skinheads." The cymbals and percussion that open the track are also used to open the show. The audience hears cymbals and percussion in lieu of the actual sound made by Noah's body hitting trees and forest underbrush. Perhaps most striking is the looping of West's hollering and staggered breathing from "Black Skinheads," which symbolizes Noah's breathing.

West's succinctly placed hollers parallel Noah's growing anxiety and frustration about finding a literal and figurative way out of the woods. As Noah hides, the background accompaniment completely fades out and only the breathing is heard on the track as the audience watches Noah's eyes frantically scan the landscape for the patroller or his dogs. The accompaniment breathes for Noah when he can't breathe for himself. In another part of the scene, viewers listen to a pounding percussion and synthesizer accompaniment as Noah pushes his nose against his shirt to hide his breathing. The percussion and synthesizers represent Noah's pounding heartbeat. Further, while Noah attempts to silence himself, the viewer is reminded of the direness of his situation via the hip-hop track.

The scene also highlights particular verses from West's track that imagine both West's known emphasis on hypermateriality and Noah's race to freedom away from being a piece of property. The intentional (dis)placement of West's lyrics to narrate Noah's failed attempt to escape slavery are significant in that they bridge two culturally recognizable representations of black life: hip-hop and slavery. Further, the slight but recognizable background noises of what a slave chase might sound like—baying dogs, breaking twigs, and the faint tinkle of the escape wagon's bell—bleed into the loudness and abrasiveness of the hip-hop track. The sonic realism of the disruption of the forest by the slave patroller's pursuit and Noah's flight paired with West's lyrics as a mocking narration of Noah's attempt to escape signifies upon the anachronistic approach of how contemporary (black) viewers believe they might act in a similar situation.

The use of "Black Skinheads" and other hip-hop music in the *Underground* series is unexpected and jarring to the ear because of the immediate recognition of a contemporary sound to sonically annotate an otherwise historically entrenched moment of black life. The first season of *Underground* is set in 1857 Macon, Georgia, while songs like "Black Skinheads" were released in 2013. The large temporal chasm between the historical time periods of nineteenth- and twenty-first-century black experiences is bridged by hip-hop. The inclusion of twentieth- and twenty-first-century black music to accompany Noah and his group's attempt to escape slavery moves beyond being a mere way to engage a younger generation of viewers. Rather, hip-hop serves as an entry point for witnessing the horrors and complexities of enslaved black people trying to maneuver the white supremacist power structures historically documented in the American imagination. while plotting their own sense of freedom and agency. In essence, the sonic elements of hip-hop—both rappers' voices and their instrumental accompaniments—are used to validate the traumatic lives of enslaved blacks.

I use hip-hop to annotate southern blackness as my entry point into this discussion because few studies address the way hip-hop buoys representations of southern black life. The crux of hip-hop and hip-hop studies is dominantly northeastern and urban. Yet popular reimaginings of slavery, such as *Underground*, and other revisionist renderings of emancipatory narratives, such as *Django Unchained*, are set in the rural American South and use hip-hop to sonically and culturally centralize a traumatic black experience. I am interested in moving past hip-hop's sonic aesthetics as a lure for contemporary consumers of popular culture to engage slavery as a southern black experience. Evoking contemporary sounds of black life and agency like hip-hop ruptures the visual representations of slavery offered to a contemporary multicultural audience. Hip-hop lifts the slave narrative in a way that simultaneously tugs at and pulls away from the trauma of the slave experience. For example, the visual keystones of a modern retelling of a slave narrative—the Southern plantation, tattered clothes, and dialect (in some instances sloppily extended for an immediate recognition of *southernness*) remain in place. The sonic backdrop and other aural accompaniments are not tethered to historical boundaries. Although subtler in its purpose—I do not want to mistake subtlety for volume—the sonic aesthetics of slave narratives are ripe for questioning how sociocultural renderings of slavery remain the anchor and wall for navigating scripts of Southern black agency and experience.

In popular culture's presentation of slavery to a mainstream audience, hip-hop serves as a tool of what Fred Moten describes in his book *In the Break* as "defamiliarizing the familiar."[1] The use of hip-hop in performing slave narratives not only destabilizes the cultural markers assigned to slavery and its residual effects but also "illuminate[s] the terror of the mundane and quotidian rather than exploit the shocking spectacle."[2] Mainstream historical renderings of slavery are indeed shocking, in their focus on the rash and more pronounced physical violence associated with enslaved black bodies. Considering this current hypertraumatic sociocultural landscape that black Americans attempt to navigate, "contemporized" slave stories become an extension of the familiar reality of lagging black agency. Still, the more subtle and often overlooked aesthetics of slavery's lasting impact—that is, the sonic—provide an alternative method for engaging slavery's lasting effects on the sociocultural markers of black life in America. I am interested in teasing out how hip-hop's audiovisual aesthetic grounds the reading and consumption of slave narratives. For example, how do the sonic markers of hip-hop heard in Quentin Tarantino's film *Django Unchained* amplify and destabilize the American South as a space of reckoning for fugitive slaves and their desires to imagine themselves free? I am also interested in Edward P. Jones's novel *The Known World* and how his rendering of black slave masters pushes past an alternative, difficult composition of Southern blacks as strictly victims. These present-day sonic retellings of slavery occupy an anachronistic popular space where race and identity politics found in popular discourses collide with historic truths. This essay seeks to tease out how hip-hop aesthetics provides context for engaging slavery as a physical, cultural, and sonic space of (southern) black identities.

Hearing and Signifying upon the Unimaginable: Sounding Slavery in Popular Culture

Growing up on the rural side of south Albany I was surrounded by plantation life and culture. It wasn't until I was older and in graduate school that I started paying attention to how heavily invested the South remained in plantations, especially near my grandparents' home: the small, often rickety metal signs plastered against ranch-style metal fences that warned against trespassing or pointed to plantation service entrances; the quaint wooden cottages and massive oak trees dressed in moss that dotted the front entrance of the plantation hid rings of trailers or shotgun houses with stout front porches where the bus would drop us kids off from school. Then vice president Dick Cheney hunted quails in nearby Thomasville on the historic Coalson née Melhana Plantation and it made the evening news.

Plantation tourism is big business in the South. It is propelled by what Tara McPherson calls the "nostalgia industry": people visit plantations to experience the life enjoyed by planters and their families in the antebellum South.[3] Tours, weddings, and historical reenactments keep many towns and small cities in the South in business. In Georgia, for example, a "Road to Tara" billboard campaign attracts customers who are interested in *Gone with the Wind* and its setting, Tara Plantation. As Karen L. Cox writes in *Dreaming of Dixie*: "The South of the imagination was, and still is, very often created by the industries of popular media. . . . It was portrayed as a place where those traditions still had meaning, and where Americans, if they ventured South, might get to experience the Dixie of their dreams."[4] It is important to note that Dixie as "the South" offers a selective, white rendering of the South. Dixie is grounded in the antebellum plantation, a physical and cultural space that is sold as a universally southern concept but is a racially splintered relic of Southern identity. For example, the upkeep of plantation homes to sustain the visual splendor of their white columns, large porches, and groves of pecan and fruit trees conveniently boxes out the less-than-splendid reality of how the visual beauty of the plantation came to exist in the first place. Slaves are conveniently overlooked as the means by which planters and their families enjoyed the luxuries of antebellum life. Their narratives are removed from tours or watered down to avoid casting planters and their families in a less-than-positive light. Selective memory of plantations as ethical farms filled with happy black workers stabilizes plantation narratives and ultimately tourists' qualms about slavery, thus positioning the plantation as the root of collective memory for life in the South.[5]

It is in this rendering of the plantation as a metaspace that popular culture situates its understanding of the South. The comfort of what Zandria Robinson argues is an "imagined plantation past" produces a complicity surrounding (southern) black agency that is valued and upheld in America's mainstream popular imagination.[6] There is no room for blacks to question their discomfort with or dismissal of the plantation as a site of agency. Saidiya Hartman's theorization of "roots tourism" in her essay "The Time of Slavery" highlights the messiness of situating slavery in voyeuristic depictions of post–civil rights popular culture: "Yet, what does it bode for our relationship to the past when atrocity becomes a commodity and this history of defeat comes to be narrated as a story of progress and triumph? If restaging scenes of captivity and enslavement elide the distinction between sensationalism and witnessing, risk sobriety for spectacle, and occlude the violence they set out to represent, they also create a memory of what one has not witnessed. The reenactment of the event of captivity contrives an enduring, visceral, and personal memory of the unimaginable."[7]

The danger in re-creating the "unimaginable" aspects of slavery without proper context is the risk of losing the agency associated with that culturally traumatic memory. The loose and polarized rendition of the plantation as the crux of understanding slavery parallels its position as not only a commodified space but also a fetishized memory of white supremacy. The unimaginable slides into the margins and occupies space in other lesser recognized avenues of popular cultural production. The unimaginable is often sonic: the screams of enslaved women and men as they are raped; the sighs and huffs caused by overworked black hands, backs, and chests; the sound of baying dogs and slave patrollers' excited laughter as they incite their dogs to tear into fugitive slaves' bodies.[8] The work of annotating slavery's horrors often falls on the recognition and use of sound to lay claim to the fact that slavery was truly horrific. Sonic renderings of slavery, paired with sonically recognizable black music such as hip-hop makes room for an alternative imagining of a slave plantation to complicate its associated racial identity politics.

Consider Quentin Tarantino's 2012 slave revenge fantasy *Django Unchained*. Tarantino is no stranger to controversy or violence, the latter being a cornerstone of his body of work. *Django* stars Jamie Foxx as the former slave turned bounty hunter, Django Freeman; Christoph Waltz as his German partner, King Schultz; and Leonardo DiCaprio as Calvin Candie, a rich Mississippi planter who fights male slaves in "mandingo" fighting across the pre–Civil War South. After being forcefully freed by Schultz, Django sets out to find his wife Broomhilda, nicknamed Hildy, played by Kerry Washington. Hildy signifies black exceptionalism—she is fluent in German because of her first owner. Yet Hildy also signifies upon the term "trophy wife," attractive and literally and figuratively a prized possession for both Django and Candie.

Yet *Django*'s use of hip-hop and popular black music is central to the tale of a good slave gone bad. The undeniable presence of the voices of Tupac Shakur, Rick Ross, and James Brown buoy Django as the ultimate black macho, a performative hyperblack masculinity that transcends temporal and cultural boundaries. The distinct sonic touchstones of hip-hop masculinity offered in the film's soundtrack suggest that violence against male slaves and their revolt is generational and a residual place keeper. To borrow from Mark Anthony Neal, the otherwise illegible masculinities of enslaved black men are made legible using hip-hop.[9] Django's manhood is wrapped up in the recognition of the masculinity of black male performers like Shakur and Rick Ross. Specifically, a particular type of black masculinity is rendered hypervisible—the anxiety and adamant desire for respect heard in hip-hop and funk music. Simultaneously, the use of black popular music in *Django Unchained* reifies the stereotypical beliefs about black masculinity while attempting to reclaim the voice of enslaved black men otherwise overlooked in the popular imagination.

"Unchained," a mash-up of Tupac Shakur's lyrics from his posthumous release "Untouchable," is set against an instrumental sample from James Brown's "The Payback" that highlights Brown's signature holler and horns. The mash-up signifies Django's transition from slavery to freedom, with Brown and Shakur sonically narrating his emotional response. "Unchained" captures Django's conversion from enslaved black man to free black male bounty hunter in one long sonic stride. James Brown's voice substitutes for Django's own as Brown's lyrics are used to narrate his anger as a slave: "Sold me out for chump change . . . told me that they . . . had it all arranged."[10] Shakur's menacing and emphatic question "Am I wrong 'cause I wanna get it on til I die?" is set against the loudness of the horns and electric guitar from Brown's live band.[11] The horns signify Django's arrival and his hell-bent search for his wife—the ultimate form of revenge and marker of humanity. Still, Django briefly speaks for himself, with a looped sound bite of Foxx/Django telling his former overseer "I love the way you die boy" in response to Shakur's voice. Foxx's voice signifies upon the possibility of how a slave might avenge himself with a soundtrack. This is an intriguing parallel to other documented but aurally silent slave revolts like Nat Turner's 1831 rebellion in Virginia. "Unchained" brings Django's anger and position as an enslaved man to life. Hip-hop and funk present the unimaginable: Django's ability to carry out and find pleasure in revenge.

Django's search for Hildy steers him to Candie's plantation, Candieland, located in Mississippi. After Schultz and Django convince Candie they are in search of slave fighters, Candie invites them back to his plantation. Candieland is a visually stunning landscape of lush trees and well-manicured fields and lawns. The name evokes the innocence of the childhood board game Candyland as well as the brutalities of slavery that propped up Candieland's grandness.[12] Django is positioned as a black slaver who needs to conceal the fact that he once was enslaved. He rides on a horse as Candie's new slave fighters walk behind him. When Candie's white workers taunt Django, he asserts himself as a man and threatens violence. It is in this scene from *Django Unchained* that the audience hears Rick Ross rap across a track titled "100 Black Coffins." After a sound bite plays from the scene where Django defends his manhood, a lone whistler, wailing chorus, and the sound of hissing air and clinking iron start on the track. The whistle, chorus, and clinking allude to the sonic backdrop of spaghetti westerns and the underlying notion of industrialism and railroads. With the addition of Ross's voice, however, I would suggest that the sound of clinking chains alludes not only to slavery but also to the chain gang, a cheap form of labor that takes hold during Reconstruction. If one is reading *Django* as a measurement of popular black masculine expression, Ross is an intriguing inclusion on the soundtrack considering the controversy around his street credibility as a former correctional facilities officer (which adds yet another layer evoking the transmittance of slavery using hip-hop's connection to the prison industrial complex). Ross opens his verses with references to multiple types of black subjects—preachers, bibles, and coffins. He also performs call-and-response with himself, a signifier of the Baptist oral tradition rooted in the South. While there is an awareness of the gospel tradition, Ross intentionally and violently subverts these images to establish his own sense of agency. Ross blends contemporary imagery associated with hip-hop—hustling, street knowledge, and drug culture—with historical markers of violence against enslaved blacks. Whether intentionally or inadvertently, Ross situates pathological markers of black masculinity side by side. Ross's performance pairs the perceived threat of enslaved men as dangerous with the audience's expectation of hip-hop masculinity as equally menacing. Sound blurs these historical and cultural paradigms of black masculinity together to complicate where the historical reckoning of slave masculinity ends and contemporary tangling with black men begins. Because this pairing takes place lyrically and sonically, there is room to question but not centralize the problematic renderings of angry black men.

Ross's track foreshadows not only the outcome of the film's plot but also perhaps the most gruesome point in the film, the murder of Candie's mandigo fighter D'Artagnan. D'Artagnan attempts to run away but is captured and brought back to Candieland the same day Django and Schultz arrive. The slave begs for his life and forgiveness, claiming that he is tired of fighting but undefeated. With a smile on his face, Candie orders that D'Artagnan be torn apart by dogs. His white overseers happily oblige, hooting and hollering as D'Artagnan's screams and ripping flesh can be heard among the sounds of snarling dogs. The camera never pans to D'Artagnan's dying, focusing instead on the soundscape of his death and the reaction of Django and Schultz witnessing the slave's murder. Django appears calm and does not break character. He has witnessed violence against slaves his entire life. Schultz, however, appears sickened and horrified as a result of being unable to buy the man from Candie and seeing the realities of slave life and death in vivo. D'Artagnan's death haunts Schultz until his own demise onscreen. Candie immediately notices that Schultz is "green around the gills" and grows suspicious of him. Django quickly comes to Schultz's defense and Candie seems appeased.

Unlike Tarantino's use of animated and fantastic violence in his other films, his portrayal of D'Artagnan's death is a visually subtle but wracking moment of reckoning. Christina Sharpe writes in *Monstrous Intimacies*, "The everyday violences that black(ened) bodies are made to bear are markers for an exorbitant freedom to be free of the marks of a subjection in which we all are forced to participate."[13] The use of sound to witness D'Artagnan's death signifies upon the viewer's inability or refusal to reckon with the very real horrors of slavery's brutality. It provides a moment of historical clarity and accuracy that is otherwise overlooked in the rest of the film. Further, Schultz's reaction to D'Artagnan's death and Candie symbolizes the nonsouthern viewpoint of slavery and white Southerners as monstrous. The quiet monstrosity of slavery in the South was viewed as normal by white Southerners and unrecognized if not silenced in favor of upholding Southern heritage.

Additionally, there is also the very real possibility of the underlying eroticism of attraction to slave men, a doubly taboo subject in the antebellum South. The consumption of D'Artagnan's body—the dogs' eating his flesh and the spectacle of his death—speaks to the even more subtle horrors of what Vincent Woodward defines as the "delectable Negro." Woodward's definition of "delectable" offers a useful context for exploring D'Artagnan's death: "The desire for the African slave or American black had epicurean implications. This desire was less about literal consumption and more about the cultivated taste the white person developed for the African."[14] D'Artagnan's death was a delectable experience for Candie: his pleasure in tearing a black man apart on a whim speaks to the larger underlying culture of *power* and *violence* as combined pleasurable practices for white planters.

This One Black Back: Rendering Contemporary Slave Identity Politics in *The Known World*

The author Edward P. Jones's 2003 novel *The Known World* sparked conversation about the displacement of slavery in America's post–civil rights popular imagination. *The Known World* chronicles the history of slavery in fictional Manchester County, Virginia, and excavates the narratives of black slave owners. Unlike previous renditions of slavery found in novels like Toni Morrison's *Beloved* (1987), Ishmael Reed's *Flight to Canada* (1976), Gayl Jones's *Corregidora* (1975), or Sherley Anne Williams's *Dessa Rose* (1986), *The Known World* forces the reconsideration of slavery within the black community as strictly a site of victimhood and traumatization. A significant element of Jones's push past traditional slave narratives is the southern world-building that takes place throughout the novel. Jones stated in an interview that he provided Manchester County, Virginia, with census records to specify "a hard background of numbers and dates that makes the foreground of the characters and what they go through more real." Jones's creation of "data" to root his characters suggests an awareness of slavery as not only a sociohistorical experience but also an empirical narrative. He situates

Manchester County within the American South and the town itself be-comes a character central to the story. Jones's creation of Manchester County falls into what Thadious Davis recognizes as a "southscape," a radical reenvisioning of southern spaces that centralize blackness.[15] Jones uses the novel's setting to move past the social, political, and his-torical rigidity of actual sites of slavery and exercise his reordering of slave life and culture as an act of reclamation.

Additionally, Jones indicates an awareness of the messiness of con-temporary racial politics. In a 2008 interview with Maryemma Graham, he speaks about hip-hop as a problematic site of blackness and profit that inspires my discussion of grounding *The Known World* within what I theorize as a critical hip-hop sensibility:

> It is as if slavery were legal. Something happened to black people in the '80s. We see it all the time: You can pick out some of the worse rap stars and you know what they would do . . . you can see it now. It would be one of those BET or MTV music awards. There is a runway outside, red carpet, and since slavery is legal, some guy would show up and there would be a strap, and chains would be connected to black people. He would have a turban on, dressed with all his fine clothes, and gold everywhere, the bling-bling; the gold chains are connected to his ten slaves. Then somebody says, "Silver P, you are good looking tonight." Then Silver replied, "I got all my niggers here. See Sam here, he cost $25,000, but he's worth it. He shines shoes like I don't know what."[16]

While Jones does not elaborate on the "something [that] happened to black people in the '80s," his example points to the inculcation of hip-hop in black cultural consciousness during that decade. Jones's response suggests an awareness of hip-hop as a springboard for post–civil rights black identities. Jones depicts hip-hop as strictly—or even blindly—capitalistic. It is an often unspoken recognition that recent generations of black people seek out economic signifiers of worth no matter how absurd or regressive. Jones hones in on hip-hop as a tool of black people's corruption without paying attention to the repercussions. He blends hip-hop's promise of glamour and prestige via the mantra "hustle by any means" with the historical justification of enslaving black people in the United States. Particularly striking is his invocation of hip-hop in his creation of an imaginary South that confronts slavery as the foun-dation of contemporary (southern) American blackness. Jones's need for an imaginary world parallel but not one wed to the physically tan-gible South is a point of departure for how he uses contemporary black agency to push back against the sanitary and flat understanding of slavery as Southern, white supremacist, and racially polarized.

It is Jones's description of hip-hop slavery within the hypervisible mediums of BET and MTV, however, that solidifies the need for a reconsideration of slavery in this contemporary moment. While BET continues to signify black essentialism, Jones's inclusion of MTV likely demonstrates his awareness of the 2003 incident where the rapper Snoop Dogg uses two black women in dog chains as a red carpet prop. Jones's reference to MTV demonstrates an awareness of hip-hop's crossover as a multicultural commodity. His description destabilizes slavery and hip-hop as primary touchstones of a black American identity while blending the discourses together to speak to African American trauma as a commodifiable space. Both slavery and hip-hop serve as spaces of collective memory and capitalism. Jones's prose suggests a recognition of his position as a keeper of collective cultural memory. His rendition of slavery by including black slave owners in *The Known World* creates space to bridge slavery's present and historic tensions. I do not suggest that Jones set out to write a hip-hop slave novel. Rather, I do suggest that hip-hop informs his negotiations of slavery as a reflection of not only black identity but contemporary black southernness. As Salamishah Tillet argues in *Sites of Slavery*, "the past is neither stable nor fixed but a malleable subject that present-day writers and artists can reappropriate, reconstruct, and reclaim. In many ways, the post-civil rights depictions of slavery are examples of a post-modernist practice, for they employ the formal techniques of fragmentation, intertextuality, and discontinuity, while also engaging in the deconstructionist critiques of the totalizing narratives embedded in American law and civic culture."[17] Thus, using contemporary black aesthetics to situate slave narratives like *The Known World* creates room to renegotiate slavery as an (a)historical discourse that reflects the limitations of racial politics currently in place.

Jones's emphasis on "the bling-bling," "gold everywhere," and the rapper/slave owner's name Silver P provides hip-hop as a contemporary context in situating enslaved blacks as a by-product of materialistic pursuits of racial enterprise. I'm particularly struck by the southernness of the terms Jones invokes in his parodying of slavery using hip-hop. "Silver P" evokes the New Orleans rapper and founder of No Limit Records Percy "Master P" Miller, and Jones's use of "bling-bling" is a direct reference to the burgeoning appeal and turn in hip-hop to the South via New Orleans–based Cash Money Records and their artist BG's song "Bling Bling." In tandem with Jones's parodying of hip-hop using the South, Sarah Mahurin Mutter's theorization of "thingness" and slavery in her essay "'Such a Poor Word for a Wondrous Thing'" provides further useful context in framing Jones's conceptualization of slavery within commercial hip-hop. Mutter writes: "Thingly humans are best understood in their relation to everyday material items, to other commodities . . . when people are equated with commodities—objects to be used by other people—the elusive qualities that comprise 'humanity' fall away; their conversion to thing is solidified."[18] Mutter's conceptualization of slaves as "thingly humans" translates as a double entendre within a commercial hip-hop premise; the thingness of slaves correlates with the commodification of rappers. A particularly striking example of this duality is the description of Sam, Silver P's shoe shiner. Sam's thingness as a shoe shiner parallels the commodification of Silver P's blackness within commercial hip-hop. Jones annexes Sam's working status as a slave within the hip-hop working-class aesthetics that dictate contemporary black authenticity.

Tillet argues that post–civil rights black artists attempt to reclaim the right to "formally remember slavery" and "democratize U.S. memory."[19] In shaping slavery as a tangible cultural memory, Tillet suggests that slavery transcends its historical context and connects with more contemporary challenges like poverty and other forms of socioeconomic displacement seen in hip-hop. *The Known World* remises slavery and exposes the racial anxieties that blacks currently face in this imagined postracial era. The search for inclusion in the national narrative or what Tillet calls a "democratic aesthetic" allows us to see how hip-hop and a novel like *The Known World* are in political conversation. Although hip-hop is the most visible and commodified form of blackness to date, the subjectivity and malleability of black bodies within the U.S. sociocultural landscape, especially in the South, highlights the extant marginalization of and disenfranchisement of blacks. This peculiarity is historicized in *The Known World*, as the novel provides a nuanced lens into the implications of slavery upon one's self and a black collective conscious. In his narrative, the character Henry Townsend, for example, points to the inaccuracy of imagining slavery as a polarized site of white privilege and black victimization.

Henry is born a slave but after his freedom is purchased by his father falls under the tutelage of his former master William Robbins. Ironically, Henry's slave owning does not supplement his own ownership by his father Augustus: "Augustus would also not seek a petition for Henry, his son, and over time, because of how well William Robbins, their former owner, treated Henry, people in Manchester County just failed to remember that Henry, in fact, was listed forever in the records of Manchester as his father's property."[20] Because Henry's view of slavery relies upon his blindness to the (im)morality of slavery—"Nobody never told me the wrong of that"—Henry does not consider himself or slavery to be corrupt.[21] Henry's outlook on slavery not only reflects Robbins's influence but the impossibility of his being corrupted by slavery because of his status as a former slave. He vows to "be a master different from any other, the kind of shepherd master God intended."[22] In her essay "Imagining Other Worlds," Katherine Clay Bassard writes of Henry: "That Henry grows up in a system where property relations are recognized above family relations constitutes the construction of his identity and his world. While Augustus' 'ownership' of Mildred and Henry are of the benevolent kind, Henry grows up 'free' to participate in commercial slave owning. In Henry's world, the categories of bond and free, while often racially connected, also constitute the power line that at times renders the color line problematic and moot."[23] Bassard's theorization of the power line, a remix of W. E. B. Du Bois's "problem of the color line" from *The Souls of Black Folk*, is a palpable lens in understanding Henry's investment in power as a racially neutral discourse.[24] Bassard defines the power line as "a slippage in subjectivity that occurs when identities shift from one side of the social text of power to the other in such a way as to cause a temporary destabilization in the coordinates of the oppressor and the oppressed."[25] In this sense, Henry's previous subjectivity as a slave destabilizes his narrative as a slave owner. His performance of blackness is dictated not by his or his parents' narratives as slaves but by the possibility of transcending slave narratives by becoming a slave owner. Henry centers his blackness in the flawed logic of slave ownership as an act of empowerment and economic and cultural comeuppance.

Henry's outlook on slavery as a subversive narrative of power is substantiated by the perceptions of slavery that Robbins imposes upon Henry during his "tutelage." Upon buying his first slave Moses, for example, Henry initially treats him as an equal, a member of his entourage. Henry's treatment of Moses can be read similarly to that of a rapper's treatment of his crew early in his career. Fellowship between the two men, that is, "tussling," exhibits a mutual appreciation. Yet in a defining moment of Henry's mastery, Robbins deflates Henry's affection for Moses after viewing the two men "playing like children in the dirt."[26] Appalled, Robbins summons Henry to him—like a master beckons a slave—and Henry obliges. Without direct eye contact Robbins reprimands Henry about his ignorance of the slave/master dichotomy, giving a brief monologue on the powers and limitations of slave ownership:

> "Henry," Robbins said, looking not at him but out to the other side of the road, "the law will protect you as a master to your slave, and it will not flinch when it protects you . . . but the law expects you to know what is master and what is slave. And it does not matter if you are not much darker than your slave. The law is blind to that. You are the master and that is all the law wants to know. The law will come to you and stand behind you. But if you roll around and be a playmate to your property, and your property turns around and bites you, the law will come to you still, but it will not come with the full heart and all the deliberate speed that you need. . . . You are rollin around now, today, with property you have a slip of paper on. How will you act when you have ten slips of paper, fifty slips of paper? How will you act, Henry, when you have a hundred slips of paper? Will you still be rollin in the dirt with them?"[27]

Robbins depicts slave law as colorblind and nonpartial. Unlike Henry, however, Robbins's status as a wealthy white slave owner *does* make the law impartial to him. He has no difficulty discerning his narrative from property because he *owns and dictates* both narratives. White (patriarchal) privilege is only rendered visible to him through Henry's misuse of power. Henry, however, must still combat his identity as "Nigger Henry" and fight past slave experiences to rise to the bar of the law's colorblindness. Indeed, Henry must be willing to invoke white supremacist privilege in order to distinguish himself as a slave owner, not a *black* slave owner. Therefore, after Robbins's rebuke, Henry performs what he views as "good ownership" by physically assaulting Moses. He repeatedly slaps Moses for "talking back" about the amount of work that could be done for the day by both men.

David Ikard speaks to the racial calculus of ownership: "In such an ideologically warped milieu where African Americans are socially conditioned to see white dominance and the brutal exploitation of black bodies for cultural gain as natural, the emergence of African American slaveholders becomes a radical indictment against white supremacist ideology."[28] Ikard's identification of slavery as a "warped milieu" of white supremacist discourse locates where these traumatic racial experiences take place. He credits Jones's use of setting as the novel's primary site of slavery as cultural trauma, frequently using the setting as a nuanced complement to the literal critique of white supremacy Jones provides throughout the text. After leaving Moses to work by himself for the rest of the day, for example, Henry listens to his surroundings: "He heard the sounds of Moses working. The birds of the day began to chirp, and in little more than a mile, the bird songs had replaced completely the sound of the man working behind him."[29] The description of birds chirping while Moses worked sonically reifies Robbins's interpretation of normative slave/master discourse. Chirping birds, a signifier of a bright and normal day, drowns out Henry's abuse of Moses. This scene literally and figuratively speaks to Ikard's observations of "the brutal exploitations of black bodies for cultural gain as natural." As Ikard observes, Henry's desire for economic and social equality is cloaked in his complicit acceptance of Robbins's slave/master discourse. It is in this passage that Henry attempts to distinguish himself as Moses's superior, leaving him behind as a slave instead of a peer.

Yet it is Moses's reaction to Henry's assault that best illustrates the lopsidedness of the novel's fault lines of power: "Moses felt himself beginning to sink in the dirt. He lifted one foot and placed it elsewhere, hoping that would be better, but it wasn't. He wanted to move the other foot, but that would have been too much—as it was, moving the first foot was done without permission."[30] We can read the sinking ground as a metaphor for slavery. Moses's response demonstrates his inability to think outside of a white supremacist construct—he's "world stupid."[31] The action of lifting one foot and placing it elsewhere alludes to Moses's belief that Henry would, indeed, be a better master because of his blackness and past slave experiences. Moses's "sinking feeling," however, illustrates his disappointment in Henry's inability to actually achieve a different, improved standard of slave ownership. After Henry slaps him, Moses is jolted back to the harsh reality that Henry may be black but his treatment of him as a slave and equal was not any better than that of Robbins, his first and white master. Slavery supersedes race and gender because of blacks' *and* whites' investment in it as a site of white supremacy. Perhaps most important is Moses's recognition of himself as property. Moses's distinction between himself and Henry vis-à-vis Henry's assault and relationship with Robbins reemphasizes Moses's "world stupid" as the foundation for slavery's success.

But Jones's most striking use of cultural trauma is his development and depiction of women's narratives in the novel. Jones's construction of powerful, independent black female characters like Alice Night (Walker), for example, provides black women the opportunity to move past slave women as strictly traumatic figures. His treatment of enslaved women in *The Known World* points to an awareness of the unspeakable sexual and psychological trauma black women endured during slavery.

Alice's worldview best encapsulates the complication of the novel's title; she manipulates constructions of consciousness to exist in a space nestled between a dominant worldview and her own self-awareness. Her worldview speaks not only to Jones's awareness of gender in slavery but also to the ideology of the writer Alice Walker. Walker's construction of strong black women characters and her concept of "womanism" is Jones's lynchpin between slavery and hip-hop aesthetics as a realignment of signifying upon blackness as a commodity. Alice reclaims her self-worth and identity by taking on the "willful" and "courageous" performance of madness in order to cope with the patriarchal restrictions of slavery. Similarly to Walker's character Sophia feigning weakness in the wake of her imprisonment due to racism in Walker's novel *The Color Purple*, Alice understands that the need to stay in character reflects the seriousness of her performance as a method of survival. Alice's devout performance of insanity reflects the risks of her being found out by Henry or slave patrollers and the literal and figurative loss of her freedom.

Described by other slaves as having "half a mind," Alice feigns madness in order to exist on the fringes of society while maintaining awareness of the world around her. Alice's insanity "has served as a mask for her shrewdness as well as a signifier of another world and alternative vision."[32] Her performance as a madwoman allows her to maneuver the peculiarities of slavery as a hypermasculine, heteronormative space. Alice's occupation of slavery as a gray sociocultural space highlights what Susan V. Donaldson argues is the "unrecognized, unacknowledged stories, alternative scripts" overlooked in conventional slave narratives.[33]

Alice is introduced as a sad, mentally ill figure because of being kicked in the head by a mule. Alice's incident connects her to the literary tradition of Zora Neale Hurston and her assertion of black women as the "mules of the world." Alice's incident provides the foundation for her mobility as a wanderer: "No one questioned her because her story was so vivid, so sad—another slave without freedom and now she had a mind so addled she wandered in the light like a cow without a bell."[34] Purchased for "$228 and two bushels of apples not good enough to eat and only so-so enough for a cider that was bound to set someone's teeth on edge," Alice's status as a "thingly human" and "damaged goods" provides her the opportunity to construct her own narrative, one that challenges the inferiority of slave women.[35] Like the bushel of apples used to buy her, Alice embodies the opportunity to "set someone's teeth on edge," juxtaposing the sexual stigmas attached to her slave woman identity with the fears of her performed madness.

This juxtaposition is best described through Alice's initial encounters with slave patrollers:

> From the first week, Alice had started going about the land in the night, singing and talking to herself and doing things that sometimes made the hair on the backs of the slave patrollers' necks stand up. She spit at and slapped their horses for saying untrue things about her to her neighbors. . . . She grabbed the patrollers' crotches and begged them to dance away with her because her intended was forever pretending he didn't know who she was. She called the white men by made-up names and gave them the day and time God would take them to heaven, would drag each and every member of their families across the sky and toss them into hell with no more thought than a woman dropping strawberries into a cup of cream.[36]

Alice's performance of madness allows her to navigate between slave women and (white) women's politics of respectability. She dictates the terms of sexuality to the men patrollers. Her willingness to grab at the patrolmen's crotches alludes to that hypersexuality and easy access surrounding slave women's bodies. Alice's description as a "night walker" illustrates not only the sexuality of her body—and the commodity culture of prostitution—but the inability to stabilize her within slave discourse because of her inherent wandering at night. Yet her madness saves her from her possible rape. She literally and figuratively becomes part of the night, "worthy of no more attention than a hooting owl or a rabbit hopping across the road."[37] Alice's performance of madness simultaneously propels her existence outside of a traditional slave narrative while sustaining her "thingness." The patrollers attempt to find humor in her craziness but remain aware of her bewitchment as a night walker. Jones writes:

> When the patrollers had tired of their own banter or when they anticipated getting their pay from Sheriff John Skiffington, they would sit their horses and make fun of her as she sang darky songs in the road. This show was best when the moon was at its brightest, shining down on them and easing their fear of the night and of a mad slave woman. . . . The patrollers heard from other white people that a crazy

Negro slave in the night was akin to a two-headed chicken, or a crowing hen. Bad luck. Very bad luck, so it was best to try to keep the cussing to themselves.[38]

Alice's performance of (in)sanity is a coping mechanism, an intentional preservation of her self-agency while providing her space to critique the normative sexual and racial politics surrounding her.

In addition to her madness, most demonstrative about Alice's critique of those sexual and racial politics is her creative expression, which includes her chanting. Alice's chants are renegotiations of slave songs. Her subversive chants—repetitive, simple, and metaphoric—provide further insight into Alice's (in)sanity.

Consider how after the death of a neighbor's baby on Christmas morning Alice chants, "Baby dead baby dead baby dead / Christmas oranges Christmas oranges Christmas oranges in the morning."[39] Alice's parallel of the baby's death with the gift of oranges signifies her understanding of slaves as chattel and little distinction between the "thingness" of the oranges and the slave body as a commodity. Mutter raises the question of thingly humans as capable of emotion because of their status as commodities: "In the world of 'human property,' the world of 'thingly' personas, how can the act of love pass between objects, between commodities?"[40] Alice's chant signifies the inherent belief of black bodies as commodities incapable of enduring trauma. The chant is a double entendre that demonstrates Alice's acknowledgment of the infant's death and the trauma in the inability to recognize the loss of the baby—and herself—outside of commodified slave discourse.

Still, Alice's re-rendering of Manchester County and Townsend plantation in a multimodal map described by Calvin, the brother of Alice's former owner Caldonia, as "a map of life," best reflects how to ground her in hip-hop sensibility.[41] Alice's use of art is connected to her critical memory of slavery vis-à-vis her nightly wandering. She renders art as a site of (re)definition and access to her humanity. Alice's maps juxtapose the woodcut map labeled "The Known World" hanging in Sheriff Skiffington's office. This map, described as "browned and yellowed" signifies the peculiarity and rigidity of slavery—and white supremacy—within (hetero)normative discourse. The outdated map, hardly "wondrous," does not describe Alice's known world. Alice's maps remix the realities of slave life that are unavailable—and frequently unknown—within white supremacy. This realization is made by Calvin, who declares that the maps invoke "matters in my memory that I did not know were there until I saw them on that wall."[42] The maps, stemming from Alice's mad

performance, are her (re)entry into human respectability. They render what Susan Donaldson articulates as "brief glimpses of the diminished sense of self and world allocated to enslaved people."[43]

In a letter to Caldonia, Calvin's vivid detail of Alice's artistic master-pieces is quoted at length:

> It is, my Dear Caldonia, a kind of map of life of the County of Manchester, Virginia. But a "map" is such a poor word for such a wondrous thing. It is a map of life made with every kind of art man has ever thought to represent himself. Yes, clay. Yes, cloth. There are no people on this "map," just all the houses and barns and roads and cemeteries and wells in our Manchester. It is what God sees when he looks down on Manchester. At the bottom right hand corner of this Creation there were but two stitched words. Alice Night. . . .
>
> I noticed over her [Priscilla's] shoulder another Creation of the same materials, paint, clay, and cloth. I had been so captivated by the living map of the county that I had not turned to see the other Won-der on the opposite wall. . . . This Creation may well be even more miraculous than the one of the County. This is one about your home, Caldonia. It is your plantation, and again, it is what God sees when He looks down. There is nothing missing, not a cabin, not a barn, not a chicken, not a horse. Not a single person is missing. I suspect that if I were to count the blades of grass, the number would be correct as it was once when the creator of this work knew that world. And, again, in the bottom of the right hand corner are the stitched words "Alice Night."[44]

The positioning of her artwork—the map of Manchester County on the Eastern wall and the map of the Townsend plantation on the Western wall—further signifies Alice's rebirth. The Eastern wall signifies Alice's new beginnings after slavery—that is, "the sun rises in the East"—and the Townsend plantation art on the Western wall signifies the end of her life as a slave—that is, "the sun sets in the West." Calvin's description of Alice's art as "wondrous" and "miraculous" signifies her self-reclamation while maintaining awareness of her memories as a slave. Calvin's recognition of Alice's art removes her from a "thingly human" to a creator. As Mutter observes:

> It is through art that Alice, the "Crazy Alice" who spends the largest part of the novel wandering over the Townsend plantation and muttering incoherently, becomes a person of "wondrous thing" vari-ety instead of a caricature, a commodity, an object whose worth is

measured in apples. As the plantation and Manchester County are reduced so they may be contained within canvas rectangles, Alice is elevated. . . . It is not until she finds art—and, through her art, her first real human condition—that Alice may be said to have fully "gotten over"—to a new Jerusalem of her own creation.[45]

Alice's creation of art provides her a means to transcend slavery while remaining aware of its existence. Her mastery of staple mediums of artistic expression—clay, painting, and weaving—signifies the complexity of her existence. Her status as creator is multilayered: she is the creator of the art, creator of her new life, and creator of the narratives of those she encountered in her past life. The stitching of her name—not a mere signature—subverts slave ownership and reifies Alice's self-ownership. The first map's lack of people signifies her solitary status and wandering. Yet it is through this solitary existence that Alice is able to discover herself and translate those experiences into her artwork.

Using hip-hop aesthetics to explore twenty-first-century depictions of slavery creates space to reconceptualize the impact of sociocultural trauma on the contemporary black American experience. Hip-hop as a frame of analysis helps contemporary audiences engage the messiness of bridging historic and contemporary cultural traumas within an unstable sociocultural landscape. In particular, the use of sound and popular culture complicates and brings attention to the otherwise overlooked elements of slavery as a day-to-day experience that sustains American understandings of southernness and racial identities in the American South.

FOUR: STILL AIN'T FORGAVE MYSELF

My Daddy, Reginald Keith Barnett, died December 21, 2004, in Albany, Georgia. Daddy was tall, with the smoothest dark chocolate skin, and a bald head that shined almost as bright as his mischievous smile. He died in a tree-cutting accident near the mouth of the road where our family lived. I remember everything about that day: I was celebrating the end of a stressful 21-credit-hour semester at Albany State University with a Snickers-flavored latte and my girlfriends Toni and Chenae at a local coffee shop. My cell phone buzzed repeatedly, urgently, with back-to-back calls from my grandparents' number, labeled "Home." When I picked up and said, "Hello?" I heard a long wail on the other end and a lot of rushed discussion. My Auntie breathlessly shared the news:

"Your daddy gone! He gone! Gone!"

"Wait, what? Where did he go?"

But she'd already hung up. I called back but got no response. The Gap Band's "Outstanding" played over the coffee shop speakers. I stared at my phone, trying to figure out where the hell my father had gone to make my folks so upset. Finally, it hit me. Slowly, coldly, with goosebumps raising on my arms and biting their way to my legs and chest. My friends were concerned. They waited for me to tell them.

"My Daddy's dead," I stammered. I blinked fiercely in disbelief, hot tears stabbing the corners of my eyes while Charlie Wilson sang, "Girl you knock me out!"

I called my then boyfriend and now husband Roy, and told him Daddy was dead. He lived in Atlanta and called out of work to drive to Albany to be with me. Roy met Daddy once the month before he died, when Roy picked me up for a movie date. Daddy lived behind us in the house my Granddaddy built with his own hands in my honor. "It's Gina Lou's house," he chuckled on one of our many home videos. Daddy jogged to the house in his favorite sweats and T-shirt and shook Roy's hand, winking at me but sternly looking at Roy.

"My E-boo is my world," he said. "You gotta promise to take care of her."

Roy, still fresh in my life, looked at me and firmly shook Daddy's hand. "I will."

Roy got in to Albany later that night, around 11:00 p.m. He followed me to my grandparents' house and we stopped in front of the house where Daddy died. No lights were on in the yard. It was dark but the smell of charred wood and something else was strong and deceiving: it smelled like a cookout just ended and the yard was trying to settle. The smell of char swirled in my nostrils and around me as I collapsed to the ground and hollered. I spent the day crying: it stripped all the pitch from my voice. My wail was low and husky. I gulped the smoky air around me and coughed, hoping to inhale the last energy of my father. Roy gently stroked my back and picked me up, and we drove to my house.

We listened to R&B well into the next morning, with Roy holding me tight to his chest until my sobs and his heartbeat synced together.

"Do you need me to stay today? I can use a sick day or something," he whispered.

"Nah. I should be okay."

I kissed him. My movement pushed the smell of smoke from my clothes into my nose and it was one of the first flashes of realization that my Daddy really was gone.

Outside, as the sun peeked cautiously over the horizon in the front yard, we leaned against Roy's champagne-colored Honda Accord. I didn't want to let him go. I needed him. Roy shielded me from the grief biting at my sides and gnawing on the lump in my throat that was another crying fit waiting to be released. The driver's-side window was down. He leaned over into the car through the window and shuffled around a mess of CDs on his passenger seat. Roy handed me Atlanta rapper T.I.'s *Urban Legend* CD.

"It might help. I know you like T.I.," he said. I looked at the bright orange and green CD and turned it over in my hands. I was numb. I shrugged. I first became familiar with Clifford "T.I." Harris in 1999 as a feature on the remix of a song called "Roll Wit Me" by the Atlanta group Co-Ed. I liked him well enough, especially after his second album *Trap Muzik* released the year before in 2003.

"I'll check it out later," I said. With one last kiss and a promise to come back on the weekend, Roy drove down our gravel driveway. I winced at each pop of a rock hitting his car's tires and undercarriage.

In the days following Daddy's death, I played *Urban Legend* endlessly. It was a respite from the swarm of people coming to the house and paying their respects. I didn't want to be bothered with condolences or the pomp and circumstance of southern black people mourning. I didn't want my grief on display—I barely had a hold on it—to "show" and what seemed like getting approval for the respectable dealing and depths of my hurt. The third night after Daddy's death, Nana Boo gently scolded me before bed because I snapped at a church member trying to hug me:

"People are just tryna show you how much they loved your daddy. They just trying to ease the way a little. Be nice."

"I don't feel nice."

"Try to be nice," she pleaded with sad eyes. I lost my Daddy, sure. But she lost her son.

Urban Legend didn't need me to be nice. The thump of the tracks, the adamant yet nihilistic affirmation of no fucks given that laced Harris's braggadocio and need to survive matched my own outlook on life at the time. *Urban Legend* pushed out the waves of anger and sadness that radiated from my own chest and spirit. Some songs, like "Stand Up," let me be angry. Others, like "My Life," let me grieve myself and my father simultaneously.

I was back in class for the spring semester two weeks after burying Daddy. In particular, Harris's track "Motivation," was my true obsession. I played the song most of the day and throughout the night because I couldn't sleep. The lightness of the flute on the track represented some sense of lightheartedness that was no longer in my life. "Motivation" was a sonic act of self-medication, with Harris being my personal self-help coach while I rapped along with him. "Anything don't kill me make me better," we rapped together, mostly through tears and the sympathetic frown of my roommate who was more R&B than hip-hop. On days I had class, Roy would call with "Motivation" playing in the background, rapping his original verse, "I said get on ya job, Gina! And go to class sugar! Motivation! Ya man said get to class, Gina! Daddy would want you in class, sugar! Motivation!" Most days Roy's remix of "Motivation" would get me to at least half-ass my way through class and other responsibilities.

It would be years before I could articulate why *Urban Legend* and other trap rap artists like Jeezy, Backbone, and Three 6 Mafia helped me work through the grief of my Daddy's death. Trap rap music wasn't confined to needing to be respectable. It encouraged listeners to live their lives on their own terms and live with the consequences of those terms. The anger and grittiness presented in trap rap and even trap aesthetics seen in writers like the Mississippi native Jesmyn Ward's discussions of the deaths of five black men who were close to her in her 2013 memoir *Men We Reaped* offer the unfiltered rawness of how poverty ravishes and warps the narratives around impoverished southern black men. Although trap rap is widely understood and celebrated as a genre of hip-hop about drug culture and "the life," I am interested in presenting an alternative reading of trap as a framework for recognizing the grief and grievances of young southern black men who feel unseen or are deemed unworthy of recognition elsewhere. Specifically, I am interested in Ward's alignment with trap culture aesthetics and Harris's performances of trap to examine how grief manifests and makes young southern black masculinity legible. Where Ward uses trap to provide a more nuanced approach to remembering and humanizing the men who come from underrepresented rural Mississippi backgrounds, Harris performs trap as a grieving space, evolving from self-grievance to remembering loved ones from his old neighborhood of Bankhead, a working-class black community in Atlanta.

Trap Muzik: A Brief Context

There is increasing interest and scholarship in trap rap and its resulting expansion/commercialization outside of its origins as a subgenre of southern hip-hop.[1] While its origins are debatable—Harris himself has claimed that he started trap—it is important to note that trap, like the southern communities that trap is rooted in, is not monolithic.[2] While I do not agree with Harris that he started trap, I do agree with him that he branded trap rap in the commercial ways we acknowledge the genre today. Trap's city of origin is debatable. For example, if you believe trap originates in the city of Atlanta, its sonic imprint is gritty, buoyed by a reliance on heavy electronic beats trademarked by producers like Shawty Redd. If you believe trap originates in the city of Memphis, credit is given to groups like Three 6 Mafia and their producer and group member DJ Paul. Memphis's trap instrumentals are tinged with the blues sound that permeates much of the black music radiating out of the city. Regardless of claims to its origins, it is the sonic accompaniment that gives trap its initial signature appeal.

For my own purposes, I define trap rap as an initial subgenre of southern hip-hop that features narratives about drug life and culture and their impact on black men in the post–civil rights era southern United States. Sonically, trap features bass kicks, synthesizers, and hi-hats. The terminology of trap as we understand it today can be traced back to as early as 1992 in the music of the Port Arthur, Texas, group UGK. Specifically, their song "Pocket Full of Stones" from the *Too Hard to Swallow* album dictates the challenges and triumphs of drug culture below the Mason–Dixon Line. "Pocket Full of Stones" with its jazz-infused accompaniment, features wailing and at times intentionally squeaking horns that sonically symbolize the relentless grind of hustling drugs. Many trap artists, including Harris, reference "Pocket Full of Stones" in their lyrics. "Pocket Full of Stones" could be considered proto-trap, an initial venturing by southern rappers into what northeastern hip-hop recognized as "corner music" or drug-pusher rap.

The city of Atlanta plays an integral role in a burgeoning trap rap genre. Many artists from Atlanta spoke about drug life and culture, such as Kilo Ali's song "Cocaine" in 1990. However, it wasn't until the Goodie Mob member Khujo Goodie explicitly described the grinding down of trap culture on the bodies and spirits of young black men in the song "Thought Process" on their 1995 album *Soul Food* that the concept of the trap as we understand it today took shape. Khujo does not sensationalize the consequences of being in the trap, describing it as a necessity for survival instead of glorifying the hustle of drug culture in Atlanta. Khujo Goodie offers a pained and frustrated verse about the consequences of being pushed to the edge without any healthy options to vent or thrive as a young working-class black man. This verse is an act of self-grieving and making room to articulate a range of emotions that are rarely available for black men. In the same thread as "Thought Process," OutKast also describes and offers a warning about trap life, with Big Boi warning to avoid the trap unless you have some kind of connection—all puns intended here—to the trap because it's dangerous. On the track "Wheels of Steel" on the 1996 *ATLiens* album, Big Boi gives the listener rules about how to survive the trap if it is unavoidable. Big Boi offers further commentary on the trap in the song "SpottieOttieDopalicious" on the 1998 *Aquemini* album and the song "Snappin' and Trappin'" on the 2000 *Stankonia* album. Further, another Dungeon Family collective member, Backbone, released his trap album *Concrete Law* about trap life in Atlanta in 2001. His album was released four months before Harris's first album, *I'm Serious*.

Jermaine Dupri's So So Def All Stars collaboration also recognized the trap in Atlanta through V.I.P. Squad's song "What the F$@k" on the *So So Def All Stars Volume 3* in 1998. V.I.P. Squad's take on the trap is more lighthearted than OutKast or Goodie Mob. They present the trap as somewhere to hustle and make money so the hustle can fund the partying that will take place later. It is one of the earliest renderings of trap's close proximity to nightlife, a trend that will be picked up by future generations of trap rappers like Migos.

Today, trap is an international sensation, manifesting in popular and industrial culture—such as trap brunches, trap yoga, and trap karaoke—to musical genres from K-Pop to the hybridization of other southern musical genres like country music. One of the more recent crossover successes is Lithia Springs, Georgia, native Lil Nas X's parodic and catchy runaway 2019 hit single "Old Town Road." "Old Town Road" is a blend of country yodel and trap beats produced by the Dutch producer YoungKio. Memphis is well represented in trap with rappers like Yo Gotti, Young Dolph, and Moneybagg Yo. Atlanta remains a trap capital, boasting multiple generations of trap rappers: the influence of trap pioneer rappers like Harris, Jeezy, and Gucci Mane can be traced through their musical progeny including Future, Waka Flocka Flame, Migos, Pill, Lil Baby, and Young Thug. Atlanta also continues revising its signature trap sound with producers like Zaytoven, Southside, and Mike Will Made It.

Heavy Is the Head: Grieving and Trapping in Clifford Harris's Trap

Harris's construction of the trap differs significantly from many of his contemporaries: unlike his fellow rappers Jeezy and Gucci Mane, whose normalized if not stoic performances of trapping are as a necessary evil that has benefits, Harris presents the conceptual space of the trap as a complex space of witnessing for himself and those around him. Harris's trap is more humanistic in the sense that he uses a spectrum of vulnerability that is frequently grounded in personal and communal grieving. As Harris's celebrity increases, he leans more heavily on trap music to help navigate the pressures of hypervisibility and, to an extent, success. Harris's trap personifies multiple intersections of grieving as a coping mechanism of success, nostalgia, and visibility. His catalog outlines how he initially grieves for himself and the deaths of loved ones, climaxing with the shooting death of Harris's best friend, Philant "Big Phil" Johnson. Harris simultaneously presents the trap as a personal hell and respite from fame, an opportunity to reconnect with his original self while grappling with the price of fame and fortune.

Harris's first album, *I'm Serious*, was regionally acclaimed but was not the breakout success Harris or his team expected. The title was an adamant declaration that Harris took himself seriously as a rapper while alluding to his drug ties as a dope boy. *I'm Serious* boasted numerous celebrated producers from Jazze Pha to the Neptunes. However, the album was anchored in the vision of Harris and his fellow Atlanta native DJ Toomp, a producer with strong ties to local artists including Raheem the Dream and the New York transplant MC Shy D. Like Goodie Mob before them, Harris and Toomp crafted an Atlanta-centric album, with Harris paying homage to Bankhead. Harris's accent is thick and unapologetic, pulling from Bankhead slang and the jargon of drug culture in the city at the time.

Still, Harris paired his braggadocio with a strong sense of personal reflection, recognizing that the life he both remembered and imagined for himself through this music was dangerous, brutal, and short. His self-proclaimed moniker, "King of the South," symbolizes Harris's ability to visualize himself beyond the circumstances of his upbringing. "King of the South" can be read as a subversive allusion to the legacy of Atlanta's most well-known leader, Martin Luther King Jr., and Harris's own need to establish himself in hip-hop. By naming himself King of the South, Harris invited naysayers and supporters or "subjects" alike to engage him and his storytelling. Crowning himself the king of southern hip-hop is an exercise in self-autonomy and anticipation of death that Harris uses to make his life and experiences legible to an audience outside of the geographical and physical boundaries of Atlanta and the South. For example, the skit at the end of the song "Dope Boyz" is a performance of Harris's death, and in the following song, "What Happened?," he is having a conversation with himself and possibly with God, trying to work through why he died.

Like many young black men living in the South, Harris did not see himself living past the age of twenty-five, a sentiment expressed throughout *I'm Serious* and subsequent albums like *Trap Muzik* and *Urban Legend*.[3] Perhaps most representative of Harris's anxieties as a dope boy is the song "Still Ain't Forgave Myself." The song opens with a minimalist piano and a soft sigh from Harris, who starts the song by defeatedly telling his listeners he "still ain't forgave [him]self." Harris steps away from his braggadocio to offer a vulnerable and at times heartbreaking narrative of how he grew up. His voice is quiet and contemplative, as he tells the listener a coming-of-age narrative about how he entered the drug life at a young age while growing up in Bankhead, juxtaposing childlike innocence with grown-man realities, such as hiding his gun in his toy box. "Still Ain't Forgave Myself" is mournful in the sense that Harris mourns his lost childhood and his lack of options to make legal money. He does not shy away from the consequences of his actions, talking about being arrested for pushing drugs in his trunk. "Still Ain't Forgave Myself" is a cautionary tale that follows the trajectory of songs like Goodie Mob's "Thought Process" as a warning of what drug culture can do to destroy black men. He holds himself accountable for his own actions while describing a community in desperate need of help. Harris's socioeconomic background serves as a complement to his lifestyle, not an excuse for his decision making.

While *I'm Serious* was not a commercial success, Harris's follow-up albums *Trap Muzik* and *Urban Legend* proved to be much more successful. *Trap Muzik* set the standard for what hip-hop culture at large would view as trap rap, with Harris still offering a healthy blend of braggadocio and human reflection about his life in the trap. Whether bragging about the benefits of dope-boy life on tracks like "Rubber Band Man" or "24's," or encouraging the listener to be better than he is—"Be Better than Me"—*Trap Muzik* sets the precedent for trap rap to be accepted by a mainstream hip-hop audience. For example, the Kanye West–produced track "Doin' My Job" urges the listener to see the humanity of dope boys rather than subscribe to a flat and inaccurate misrepresentation of drug dealers strictly as criminals. One line is particularly striking, where Harris encourages his listeners to love him and others like him, stating love "won't hurt."[4] Harris's third album, *Urban Legend*, was released after his then latest stint in jail. The album reflects Harris's remorse and struggle to stay optimistic about his life while reaffirming why he was, in fact, King of the South.

As Harris began to ascend music charts, he dabbled in acting and other commercial ventures like paying more serious attention to his record label Grand Hustle. Unfortunately, Harris's change of fortune did not stop the tragic deaths of those around him, many of which are eulogized on his albums. For example, he mourns the death of childhood friends and family members in the song "Live in the Sky," featuring Jamie Foxx. The song sonically invokes a church service or funeral service, with Harris delivering the "eulogy" for multiple friends and family due to violence. Foxx softly sings behind Harris, sonically reaffirming the vulnerability of grief that Harris holds at a distance in the delivery of his lyrics. In other words, Foxx's voice is soft for Harris in ways he cannot be soft or publicly vulnerable for himself. It is important to note that Harris's roll call of deceased loved ones makes his trap a space of reckoning and visibility for those who may have died because of illegal activity. Therefore, the trap as an illicit space is made humane because of Harris's intentional remembering of friends and family that shared a similar lifestyle but succumbed to the life of trapping.

However, it is the 2006 death of Harris's best friend Philant Johnson that most impacts Harris's navigation of trap culture. Johnson is fatally wounded in a drive-by shooting that Harris believed was meant for him. The album Harris released after Johnson's death, *T.I. vs. T.I.P.*, is a jarring departure from the balance of swagger and remorse heard in his previous discography. Named after the track "T.I. vs. T.I.P." from the *Trap Muzik* album, the *T.I. vs. T.I.P.* album is Harris's performance of a split personality: the polished and spotlight ready "T.I." and the raw and unfiltered dope boy "T.I.P." Harris's splintering of his performance personas is intentional: each persona represents Harris's grappling with his celebrity and his interior pain and personality. The reemergence of Harris's T.I.P. trap-boy persona embodies the friction between rap's corporatization and its implication of the real and attached experiences of its performers. T.I.P. recognizes his displacement within commercial rap and sees T.I., not himself, as a corporate creation detached from reality. T.I.P. does not see himself as pathological but as a necessary gauge to trouble Harris's understanding and presentation of authenticity. T.I.P., threatened by commercialism because of the record label's desire to control him, finds giving up control of his experiences—selling out—problematic and resents T.I. for assumingly doing so. A trap boy refuses to affiliate with or function within a white space.

The album's opening skit, "Act I: T.I.P.," consists of a haphazard mix of media sound bites. The track portrays the media as a white hegemonic construct. It is an irremediable space for blackness and manhood. There is a blurred and often inextricable link between Harris's personal life and his rap persona. "Act I: T.I.P." touches on many of the highly publicized moments of Harris's life and career—the miscarriage of his daughter with his wife Tameka "Tiny" Cottles, his numerous court appearances and sentencings, and a repeated explication of the death of Philant Johnson. Harris's thoughts are symbolized by the incessant switching between media clips. This opening skit suggests a critical distance for the (white) consumer of Harris's work but the struggle for Harris himself to maintain distinctive boundaries between the expectation that he perform his trap persona and his personal life. Johnson's death is particularly dominant because of its constant presence across the track. The three segments presumably speak from a variety of vantage points including the album's audience, Harris's national audience, and Harris himself. The repetition of Johnson's murder implies

Harris's tremendous difficulty in digesting his friend's death. The Johnson sound bite also suggests Harris's struggle to put his grief into words. There is little discourse available for black men to discuss traumatic and violent situations.

It is T.I.P.'s heated exchange with the Warner Music Group (WMG) executive Lyor Cohen, however, that reveals T.I.P.'s true intentions. I find Harris's inclusion of Cohen in this skit particularly striking because Cohen embodies white patriarchal privilege yet is considered an integral part of hip-hop's transcendence from a marginalized African American expression to American mainstream culture. Cohen helped discover and sign rap acts like the Beastie Boys and LL Cool J. He serves as a dual portal between white (corporate) America and the hip-hop experience. Very bluntly, Cohen's background and heavy involvement in creating the present-day corporate rap scene should give him a pass. But it is the troubling exchange between T.I.P. and Cohen that unveils the complicated relationship between corporatism and black masculinity. Once T.I.P. verbally cuts his ties with corporate hip-hop, Cohen attempts to intimidate him back into a subservient role, "Listen kid, understand me here . . . you better not be playin' with my muthafuckin' money!" Cohen's threat is capitalistic and gendered. He attempts to coerce T.I.P. back into good graces by threatening his access to money.[5] Cohen's reference to T.I.P. as a kid not only denotes a lack of maturity to handle business matters but also challenges Harris's masculinity.

Cohen's intentional belittling of T.I.P.'s efforts to "emancipate" himself from the corporate status quo suggests both an ownership of Harris as a brand and the ownership of his body and how he presents himself. Unlike traditional notions of chattel slavery, Harris materialistically benefits from remaining ingrained within a white hegemonic understanding of black identity. There is an awareness of the expectations surrounding Harris and his music. Once Harris's T.I.P. persona openly acknowledges and refutes this "partnership," corporate supremacist discourse collapses and leaves whiteness exposed. Harris's struggle then becomes damage control for T.I.P.'s actions and a desperate search to find a way to maintain his access to privilege.

The confrontation at the end of the album between Harris's T.I. and T.I.P. personas is psychoanalytical warfare. Jacques Lacan's mirror stage theory proves useful in approaching the nearly schizophrenic breakdown of Harris's identity.[6] Lacan posits the mirror as symbolizing the innate understanding of self. Under normal circumstances, Harris should create his own identity based on his self-perception from the mirror. Instead, the mirror signifies a disjointed identity embodied by two distinct personalities within one communal body. The friction between the two identities is a result of extreme agitation. Because there is no room for both sets of experiences to function, T.I. and T.I.P. convene at a mirror and viciously exchange verbal blows. As T.I., Harris easily maneuvers the manufactured space set up by Cohen and WMG. Balancing corporate power and creative authority requires acknowledgment and delicate handling. T.I.P. is not a problem because he is Harris's inner badass. T.I.P. becomes a problem once he attempts to buck or challenge the system of power in place. Once Harris blurs both his commercial and personal desires and challenges, he complicates the implications surrounding the performance of his manhood and, ultimately, his humanity.

In the initial exchange, the difference between T.I. and T.I.P.'s is easily discernible. T.I. presents himself as Harris's logic, the acceptable, socially functioning representative of Harris as a public figure. His delivery is smooth, coherent, and cool. T.I.P. sees himself as a portal for Harris's legitimate rage and confronts T.I. for trying to suppress his concerns as a real nigga. T.I.P.'s tirade is angry, riddled with expletives, and on the defensive against T.I.'s interrogation. To validate his need to be present in Harris's life, T.I.P. accuses T.I. of being weak and "Hollywood," wearing suits and being fake in front of media.[7] Further, T.I.P.'s accusation, "I don't know everything but I know bullshit when I see it," alludes to the exchange in the mirror as well as to the vantage point of having an authentic viewpoint, unlike T.I. Not only is T.I.P. referring to T.I. as bullshit but he also bursts the illusion that commercial success does not come without relinquishing control of one's self. By the end of the track, there is no legible difference between T.I. and T.I.P. It is a jumble of raw emotion and chaos. T.I.P.'s reference to T.I. as Hollywood insinuates performed identity as well as an unforgivable plasticity that caters to a controlled white audience. Instead of maintaining homage to Buckhead, T.I. functions within corporate hip-hop, which in turn becomes the trap.

Perhaps most disturbing about the pseudo-schizophrenic behavior exhibited by Harris on *T.I. vs. T.I.P.* is his personification of the conflicts that are also apparent in other young Black men facing the need to perform an overextended representation of blackness. These alternative personas are necessary to work around an embedded code of silent suffering forced upon men of color to maintain mutualism in the relationship between capitalism and functionality. While Harris does not directly state that *T.I. vs. T.I.P.* is an accurate portrayal of his reality, he does acknowledge the conflicts of interests between consumption of his rap and his personal growth.

Harris works through his grief about Johnson's death on subsequent albums from "Dead and Gone" on *Paper Trail* to "Wonderful Life" on *Trouble Man: Heavy Is the Head*. "Wonderful Life" and its accompanying skit reenact the night of Johnson's death and represent Harris's striking effort to come to acceptance about Johnson's murder. The skit is vividly graphic, including snippets of conversation between Harris and members of his entourage the night of the shooting. The listeners hear gunshots and the desperate effort to wake Johnson up after he had been shot. The skit then transitions into "Wonderful Life," where Harris shares intimate conversations between himself and the deceased loved ones who matter most to him: Johnson and Harris's father. Harris shares with Johnson that Johnson's family still hasn't forgiven Harris for his death. He also promises to take care of Johnson's daughter, who he says is growing up beautifully. "Wonderful Life" is an act of forgiveness for himself, as he speaks and comes to closure with Johnson by updating him on his life after Johnson's death and how appreciative he was of their friendship.

Harris's conceptualization of the trap makes the illegibility of southern black masculinities visible and respected. Further, his navigation of trap life and culture represents the sorely misunderstood anxieties and associated grieving that young working-class black men continue to face in the present-day American South.

Men We Trapped: Jesmyn Ward's Use of Trap Rap

The writer Jesmyn Ward pulls from her roots and upbringing in DeLisle, Mississippi, to complicate the narrative around black folks in the rural South. Following a tradition similar to that of her state's literary predecessors such as Margaret Walker and Mildred Taylor, Ward eloquently weaves together both the intimate and communal spaces of southern black folks to create imaginary communities that focus on the complex interiority of southern black life and culture. While Ward is constantly heralded as William Faulkner's protégé in literary and popular criticism, it is important to move her away from a whitewashed perspective of southernness as all-encompassing and universal across time, race, and space. Rather, situating Ward in the rich African American literary tradition makes room for her writing to create new paths to the same communities that writers like Walker, Taylor, and even Richard Wright wrote about in previous eras. Faulkner is a clear influence on

Ward's writing, for example, in the active and aggressive reimagining of southern communities that do not shy away from a flawed human experience, but Ward's writing differs because it does not shrink southern black people into the backdrop or afterthought of the epiphanic arc of human experience that Faulkner provides for his white characters. In Ward's multigenre writing, southern blackness does not collapse under a white gaze or become flattened by impoverished socioeconomic conditioning. Ward's writing leans into the tough questions of how being poor impacts how black folks see the South. Her writing also reflects the anxieties of black exceptionalism that are tied to a post–civil rights era socioeconomic conditioning of poverty as a measurement of black people's humanity.

Further, Ward is in conversation with her contemporaries using southern hip-hop culture as a unifying thread in her writing. Hip-hop amplifies the understanding of the black South, even within the same state, as nonmonolithic. For example, Ward's writing connects to the coastal communities of Mississippi in a fashion similar to Kiese Laymon's writing, focusing on black communities in central Mississippi. Both writers pull from hip-hop: Laymon's use of southern hip-hop vernacular and music as an emotional catalyst for understanding contemporary black boyhood and masculinity runs parallel to Ward's use of southern hip-hop culture as an act of world-building to understand the flawed but nuanced rendering of how southern black people navigate the world around them. Unlike Laymon, who uses southern hip-hop culture to invoke a visceral response to southern black experiences, Ward uses hip-hop more cerebrally: Southern hip-hop is the grounding on which she establishes southern contemporaneity. For example, Ward's debut novel *Where the Line Bleeds* (2008) can be read using trap culture as a lens for the boys' lives: Christophe succumbs to hustling drugs while Joshua does work on the loading docks. Ward's novel is set in Bois Sauvage, the fictional coastal town that also serves as the setting for her subsequent novels *Salvage the Bones* (2011) and *Sing, Unburied, Sing* (2017).

In *Where the Line Bleeds* Ward tells a haunting tale that describes the relationship and growing pains of twins Joshua and Christophe as they come of age as young black men in post–civil rights era Mississippi. The novel opens with a description of the boys hanging out with their cousin Dunny as they contemplate jumping off a bridge, a popular pastime for teens in the town, before graduation. Ward writes: "When they were all younger, all the kids from Bois Sauvage would ride their bikes there and spend all day in a circuit: plummeting from the bridge, swimming to the shore, and then running their toes over the scalding concrete to fall to the water again. Now, the twins were almost too old to jump."[8] The leap is one of the boys' last physical representations of innocence and boyhood. The backdrop for the boys' initial transition into manhood is southern hip-hop, specifically Pastor Troy's song "Vica Versa."

"Vica Versa" is a subversive examination of southern black identities and organized religion. Sonically, the song treads a thin line between gospel music and the evolving sound of trap rap coming out of the city of Atlanta, Pastor Troy's hometown. With a gruff and gravelly voice, Troy leans into his moniker of "Pastor," offering a fire-and-brimstone reverse sermon of what faith and religion could mean for him and black men in the South. Pastor Troy's delivery is unwavering and nearly emotionless, a narrative complemented by the synthesizer and hi-hat heavy instrumental reaffirming the darkness of Troy's lyrical narrative. Perhaps most sonically vivid about "Vica Versa" is the consistent presence of a ringing church bell, an allusion not only to Troy's questioning of his faith and church iconography but also to the physical, social, and cultural death that faith is not able to help him navigate or understand. Troy's voice, paired with the prominent death knell, present a hip-hop-grafted sociocultural interrogation of faith in understanding the challenges of life and death for black southerners. Ward's use of "Vica Versa" lays the groundwork for the novel's plot concerning how young southern black men deal with the harshness of life, especially through drug dealing. The twin boys and their cousin Dunny listen to the song after jumping off the local bridge into the water, serving as multiple symbols of the ending of the boys' innocence and their "baptism" into manhood and the real world. Ward writes: "Dunny turned the music up so Pastor Troy's voice rasped from the speakers, calling God and the Devil, conjuring angels and demons, and blasting them out."[9]

Ward's use of "Vica Versa" is important for a few reasons: it foreshadows the increasing conflicts between the twins Joshua and Christophe as they navigate different life paths, signifying upon the growing strain of Joshua and Christophe's bond as twins and as black men; and it sets the stage for multiple reimaginings of black masculinity and poverty. The song also foreshadows the twins' physical and even spiritual lives being at risk, with Christophe growing distant from his family as he becomes more deeply invested in dealing drugs.

Ward's depiction of Christophe as a dope boy signifies on trap as a visceral space where the desperation of black men and boys without any viable or legal possibilities can still see themselves with options. When

Christophe drunkenly confesses to Joshua his plan to start dealing because of his inability to secure a job, Joshua tries to talk him out of it. Christophe leans into his decision, shutting down his brother's concern: "We been looking and calling for a month and I ain't got shit. I ain't got no more money left. Ain't nothing coming through. . . . What I'm going to do? Sit around and beg these fucking folks for a job and eat off of you and Ma-mee? I can't do that."[10] Ward pays intense attention to Christophe's drug dealings and his desperation to keep the ruse of him finding legal work strong enough to fool those he cares about most, his brother and their grandmother Ma-mee: "He would think of Ma-mee at the house, waiting on him, of Joshua at the dock making honest money. He would run into one of the convenience stores with a sign out on the front, grab an orange juice, snatch an application, and then drive to Bois Sauvage through the bayou and past his home."[11] Ward then vividly and painstakingly describes Christophe as a drug hustler, paying attention to how he set up his business and how he sold his product:

> He'd ride until he couldn't ignore the small red light and the constant chatter of pages through the pre-paid cell-phone at his hip. He'd reluctantly turn and go back. . . . They'd amble over at regular intervals, it seemed; alone or in pairs. Once about every hour or half-hour or so, he'd see them off in the distance. They seemed to materialize from the heat-drenched air like sudden rain. . . . He ate potato chips and drank Gatorade while he waited. . . . He waited for them to come: other drug dealers, or high school students playing hooky, or people on their lunch breaks from driving trucks hauling rocks and sand, or attendants working at convenience stations the next town over, all people he'd grown up with and always known. When they came to him, he'd shake their hands. They would joke with him, and he'd smile. He'd give them what they wanted and they'd lay the bill close to him on the table, where it would flutter and jump with the wind, where it would pulse and twitch like a living thing. One pocket was for dime sacks, the other for dubs; he'd put the money in the pocket with the dime sacks because there was more room. Feeling sick, excited, and ashamed because he was excited, he'd eye the road for dark blue cop cars.[12]

This passage is striking because of Ward's contrast between the rural countryside and the trap. Unlike Harris, who uses the urbanity of Atlanta as a backdrop to reemphasize trapping, Ward brings the trap to the rural black South, with Christophe paying attention to the otherwise quiet and isolated trap he established for himself. Sounds of nature like crickets, or natural imagery like hawks hunting for prey signify upon the otherwise slow, country life that Christophe lived outside of dealing drugs. Additionally, Christophe's clientele mostly comprised those in his community, a wide-ranging spectrum of people who invoke the different performances of familiarity and southern hospitality that Christophe provides. Christophe's labor is multifaceted: not only is he selling drugs, he's also working to keep up appearances while mourning his inability to find paying work that is legal. This passage, especially the description of Christophe's hesitancy to go to his rural trap, invokes Harris's song "Doin' My Job," where trapping is a means to an end, not a glamorized way of life.

Christophe's loss of self-autonomy and the consistent grind of selling drugs literally and figuratively eats him alive, consequences that run adjacent to the lyrics and narratives heard by trap rappers. Christophe grieves the loss of himself and the loss of his close ties to his family. Believing himself to be too far gone, he distances himself from his previous life while Joshua desperately tries to hold on. After a climactic confrontation between the twins and their father Sandman, a drug user who antagonizes Christophe, Ward ends the novel back where it began: with their cousin Dunny by the water. The boys' sense of innocence is far gone and their relationship is strained. Still, Joshua and Christophe return to each other, fishing in the local bayou, mulling over the bayou's representation of life and death and how that parallels the changes in their own lives.

The character of Christophe is fictional but the parallels between him and Ward's description of her younger brother Joshua is devastatingly familiar. Joshua was killed by a drunk driver in 2000, weeks shy of his twentieth birthday. Ward writes about the loss of him and four young men who were close to her in her memoir *Men We Reaped*. After reading *Men We Reaped* I felt left with brittle bones, as Ward's sorrow and grieving still felt fresh for her loved ones. The chapter on Joshua closes out the "obituaries" Ward painstakingly writes in tandem with her autobiographical narrative about growing up in poverty in DeLisle. Ward's description of Joshua is nuanced but complicated, steeped in the youthfulness of southern hip-hop. She does not shy away from his flaws or the complexities of his life, many of which mirror Christophe's character. Joshua struggled to find and keep a job: "My brother spent his days riding in his new car, an eighties-model Cutlass he'd bought after he accidentally shot the gas tank of his Caprice while playing with a gun. He dropped off applications at gas stations, casinos, factories."[13] When Joshua couldn't keep a job, he reluctantly resorted to drug dealing.

Ward describes watching her brother conduct a deal at their house and, after asking him outright if he did it, Joshua defends his choices, adamantly saying, "'You think I like to do this shit?' he said. 'I ain't like the rest of these fools out here. You know when I got a job, I work.'"[14] After Joshua secures a job at a local casino, he keeps his promise and is fully dedicated to being a valet.

Perhaps most striking about Ward's description of her brother is through his car. The description of the car is grounded in a southern hip-hop sensibility that is an extension of the author's description of Joshua himself. For example, early in the chapter she writes of being picked up by Joshua and their mother in New Orleans upon her return home: "[They] picked me up in the large cream-colored Caprice that my mother'd bought for herself and then given to my brother for his first car. They loaded my luggage, straining at the seams, next to the speakers in the trunk. My brother played the music low, even though he had ridiculous beat."[15] The southern hip-hop sensibilities here are loud and clear: although the car is secondhand, Joshua takes pride in the Caprice by updating it to include a loud audio system, usually including a set of subwoofers that take up all the space in the trunk. Car systems are important in southern hip-hop culture, as cars are experimental and validation spaces for if the song "knocks" or makes the car vibrate. This test, also known as the "car test," is a sacred rite of passage for many young men who are privileged to have cars. Even if the car was raggedy, the raggediness was forgiven if the car had nice speakers. Ward's description of the music being low but with a "ridiculous beat" can be read as the thrum of the bass coming from the trunk, even if the volume of the actual song itself was low. The sound of the car is significant to understanding Joshua's vibrancy as Ward nostalgically describes it. In some ways, although Joshua was unable to speak for himself, his car made his agency and autonomy known: "The sound of his car was louder than the sound of the day, the summer bugs buzzing in the trees, the electrical hum of the trailer like another larger bug."[16]

Ward's use of sound to describe Joshua's death does double duty: it reemphasizes Joshua's place in the hip-hop South and helps the author find closure by imagining his death. This type of Morrisonian archaeology—the use of imagination to fill in the gaps of unseen history and trauma of black folks—is achieved using sonic sensibilities connected to hip-hop. Ward writes: "I'd like to think it was a beautiful night, which is why he would have taken Highway 90 home. . . . He could look out of his window and see an open horizon over the water, where the waves from the Gulf quietly lapped the shore, where the oak trees in the median stood witness over centuries to wars, to men en-slaving one another, to hurricanes, to Joshua riding along the Coast, blasting some rap, heavy bass, ignorant beats, lyrical poetry to the sky, to the antebellum mansions our mother cleaned and whose beauty we admired and hated."[17] Ward's attention to sound blends the past and present, and she uses the antebellum iconography that is traumatic for southern black folks to map out the trauma of her brother's death. Joshua in his element is part of southern hip-hop, the bass coinciding with Joshua's final heartbeats, a new contribution to the black South's complicated tapestry of trauma, the triumph and joy of black folks' in-teriority in the South, and remembrance.

For Ward and Harris, trap is a space to openly grieve those who may not be seen as respectable or "worthy" of remembrance. In my own grief over my father's death, trap rap was a space to reckon with messy feelings of anger and sadness that intermingled in a less than respect-able manner. Ultimately, trap culture in southern hip-hop is more com-plicated than stories about drug dealing and the grind. It is also a space of reckoning, where a more complete depiction of the humanity of young southern black men is rendered visible.

A FINAL NOTE
THE SOUTH STILL GOT SOMETHING TO SAY

OutKast celebrated the twentieth anniversary of their first album *Southernplayalisticadillacmuzik* by going on tour in 2014. The group hadn't toured together in over a decade. I was fortunate to see them four times, once at the Counterpoint Festival in Rome, Georgia, and all three days of the OutKast ATLast music festival in Centennial Olympic Park in Atlanta. I was no longer an anxious incoming high school freshman. I was thirty and had recently completed my doctoral degree. Roy had pitched the woo and won me over forever when he told me I was his "Prototype." We were introduced to our friends and family as "Mr. and Mrs. Bradley" to OutKast and UGK's song "Int'l Players Anthem." OutKast's music was no longer a lesson in contemporary southern blackness. I was well versed by then. Still, they left an indelible mark that I refused to miss celebrating. The OutKast ATLast concerts featured southern hip-hop pioneers and newcomers alike, from acts like Janelle Monáe, 2 Chainz, and Childish Gambino to Atlanta hip-hop legends like YoungBloodZ and Pastor Troy. The third day of the festival, the "Southern Hip Hop Roundup," was the concert I most looked forward to out of all the sets of the weekend.

As I bounced my shoulders to the knock of bass coming out of Centennial Olympic Park, the person scanning my ticket frowned and pushed me into a different line. The ticket scanned as fraudulent and I was devastated. Roy had already scanned his ticket and was already in the park. I told him my ticket was fake, and he looked torn about what to say. I shrugged heavily. I'd seen OutKast two days in a row while Roy worked. I wouldn't ask him, the biggest OutKast fan I knew, to miss his chance to see them in action.

"I'll come pick you up," I pouted while Roy smiled and danced farther into the park. I waited until he was out of sight and walked the long journey back to the car. Between sobs, I pulled out my phone to talk shit about the person who sold me a fake ticket on my Facebook page. A lot of people offered their sympathy in the comments. As I drove home, I heard back-to-back alerts vibrating from my phone. I pulled over to read a series of frantic messages from my friend Gaye. She shared that her close friend was the tour manager and she asked him to get me a ticket. I called and squealed into her ear when she picked up.

"Girl, you got me a ticket?!" Gaye laughed into the phone.

"It took a bit of persuading. He thought I was trying to get you backstage."

"Girl naw my friends and 'nem are at the concert. I just want to get in."

"Go wait by Will Call," she said. "It might take him a minute to get you the ticket but he promised he would."

I wheeled my car around and sped back toward the park. After paying to park again, I ran to the ticket counter and waited for my ticket. As I waited, I danced to YoungBloodZ and Bone Crusher. Finally, the ticket counter clerk called my name and gave me my wristband. In an act of divine intervention, I happened to catch Roy and our friends standing toward the back of the park. I called out them on beat: "Aaaaaaaaye! Aaaaaaaaye! Aaaaaaaaye!" They hollered back in response. I told them about Gaye being my guardian angel. I promised her I'd babysit her kids for life. We enjoyed the rest of the night.

After the concert, I started to brainstorm about this book. I knew I wanted to write about OutKast and their significant impact on the post–civil rights era cultural landscape. By the time of OutKast ATLast, Atlanta was a stronghold of hip-hop at large. Regional affiliation was no longer the hurdle that it was in the early 1990s when Benjamin and Patton were trying to break into the industry. The hip-hop South now had multiple generations, earmarked by significant historical and cultural events like Hurricane Katrina and the rise of social media. Where Katrina physically and culturally reshaped the boundaries and intersections of southernness, social media introduced the possibility of a digital South, with young acts like Atlanta rapper Soulja Boy using the Myspace website to market his song "Crank That" to listeners around the country. The song was widely popular, one of the earliest examples of going viral in social media, and got Soulja Boy signed to Interscope Records in 2007.

Today, the South dominates hip-hop, much to the chagrin of northeastern hip-hop purists. Academically, the South is woefully underrepresented, with few exceptions, such as Darren Grem's 2006 essay "The South Got Something to Say," Maco Faniel's history of Houston hip-hop in his 2013 book *Hip Hop in Houston*, and Ali Colleen Neff's 2009 book *Let the World Listen Right* about Mississippi Delta Hip Hop. The current body of scholarship on southern hip-hop is indebted to the critical ears and writing of journalists like Charlie Braxton, Joycelyn Wilson, Maurice Garland, Christina Lee, Gavin Godfrey, Rodney Carmichael, Bené Viera, Roni Sarig, Tamara Palmer, and Ben Westhoff. It is my hope that their work and the writing of a newer crop of young black journalists coming out of the South like Yoh Phillips, DaLyah Jones, Clarissa Brooks, Brandon Caldwell, and Taylor Crumpton will be read in tandem with the increasingly rigorous academic analysis of southern hip-hop's influence on popular culture and music. When André Benjamin declared, "The south got something to say," he was rallying southern artists to speak their truths to power. Now, twenty-six years later, I would like to posit that "the South *still* got something to say." Like Benjamin in 1995, this is an adamant declaration for a growing collective of southern academics, archivists, and journalists to document southern hip-hop's legacy and influence. The South is not a monolith. The criticism that engages it should also be nonmonolithic. It is my hope that this study of OutKast and their influence is only the beginning.

NOTES

INTRODUCTION

1 In his 1964 book *Why We Can't Wait*, Martin Luther King Jr. discusses how his failures in Albany played a significant role in the way he revised his plan of action for his Birmingham, Alabama, desegregation efforts. He writes: "There were weaknesses in Albany, and a share of the responsibility belongs to each of us who participated . . . when we planned our strategy for Birmingham months later, we spent many hours assessing Albany and trying to learn from its errors. Our appraisals not only helped to make our subsequent tactics more effective, but revealed that Albany was far from an unqualified failure" (Signet Classics reprint, 29–30). See also Lee Formwalt's study of the Albany Movement and desegregation efforts across Southwest Georgia, *Looking Back, Moving Forward*.

2 Originally from College Park, a subsection of Atlanta, Pastor Troy gained popularity for his first major single "No More Play in GA" and later "This tha City," from which the line about the wicked church is pulled. Troy calls his father the "original" Pastor Troy, and says he used his upbringing in his father's church to help usher in the Atlanta hip-hop subgenre of crunk music. See Pastor Troy's interview in the "Faith Is What You Make It" episode of the Atlanta NPR podcast *Bottom of the Map* (2019).

3 See my TEDx talk, "The Mountaintop Ain't Flat," for additional discussion of the mountaintop and its relevance to the contemporary Black South.

4 George, *Post-Soul Nation*; and Neal, *Soul Babies*.

5 Robinson, *This Ain't Chicago*, 62.

6 The explanation of OutKast is provided by the fellow Dungeon Family collective member and spoken word artist Big Rube on the "True Dat" interlude from the group's *Southernplayalisticadillacmuzik* album. In an unpublished July 2019 interview with *Bottom of the Map*, Big Rube disclosed Rico Wade came up with the OutKast acronym and he expanded upon it for the interlude.

7 See the Netflix documentary *Black Godfather* and Maurice Hobson's discussion of funk music's influence on Atlanta's cultural scene in *Legend of the Black Mecca*, 205–214.

8 See the Netflix docuseries *Hip-Hop Evolution* episode "Dirty South" (season 3, episode 4).

9 Karen Marie Mason, Kriss Kross's product manager, affirmed that their southernness was not central to selling their act and brand: "I wrote and developed their marketing plan. I was not from the South and there was no real direction from [their] producer and management to focus on this. I also didn't think they could compete with what was going on musically, so my

emphasis was on the 'krossed out look,' developing them as a teen brand" (personal interview with Mason, October 6, 2019).

10 Perry, *Prophets of the Hood*, 22.

11 The mention of Atlanta as the new Motown of the South also caught my attention, as Stax Records, housed in Memphis, Tennessee, was also dubbed the Motown of the South. I am curious about whether or not this shout out was an introduction for LaFace records, established by L. A. Reid and Kenneth "Babyface" Edmonds, as an independent venture that could capitalize on Atlanta's music scene. Additionally, LaFace Records, though home to rap groups OutKast and Goodie Mob, was mostly focused on branding itself as an R&B label, boasting talent including TLC, Toni Braxton, Shanice, and Usher.

12 The rap group Goodie Mob gives attention to the Red Dog police program on the skit "Red Dog Skit" from the *Soul Food* album. The Red Dogs' vicious and militant tactics in working class neighborhoods made them infamous and highly problematic, causing the letters in the group's name to stand for "Run Every Drug Dealer Outta Georgia" in Atlanta street slang. The listener hears not only a drug exchange between members of Goodie Mob and a drug addict "Straight Shooter," but the Red Dogs' forced entry into the apartment. Straight Shooter is arguably the informant or snitch who set up the deal and led the police to the residence. The skit is an opener for the track "Dirty South."

13 I am also alluding to the southern hip-hop reference the "Dirty South," coined by the Dungeon Family member and rapper Cool Breeze. In additional to the physical renderings of the word "dirty," that is, red clay, dirt, or mud, the term also connotes the dirtiness of the treatment of southern black folks, even in the post–civil rights era, which deromanticizes the belief that the movement ended the racial and socioeconomic tensions facing southern black communities.

14 OutKast's "Welcome to Atlanta" is the first in a string of "Welcome to Atlanta" songs. The later songs, also named "Welcome to Atlanta," are produced and performed by Jermaine Dupri, the head of So So Def Records. The Dupri track, released in 2001, was set in post-Olympics Atlanta. Dupri, along with the fellow Atlanta rap act Ludacris, painted Atlanta as a party city and "the spot to be." There was a remix featuring Sean Combs, Murphy Lee, and Snoop Dogg shouting out their respective hometowns. The track was revisited in 2014, titled "New Atlanta" with a new generation of Atlanta rappers including Migos, Rich Homie Quan, and Young Thug.

15 OutKast, "Myintrotoletuknow," *Southernplayalisticadillacmuzik*.

16 OutKast.

17 For further discussion of the American South's historical tourism trade, see Cox, *Destination Dixie*; and McIntyre, *Souvenirs of the Old South*.

18 OutKast, "Git Up, Git Out," *Southernplayalisticadillacmuzik*.

19 I am not suggesting that Big Boi's verse is a criticism of his mother. It is important, however, to note Big Boi's close relationship with his aunt Renee Patton, whom he lived with when he moved to Atlanta from Savannah, Georgia. She is immortalized not only in his music but also in his live

performances during the twentieth-anniversary OutKast reunion tour. I will discuss this more in depth in chapter 1.

20 OutKast, "Git Up, Git Out," *Southernplayalisticadillacmuzik*.

21 OutKast.

22 Perry, *Prophets of the Hood*, 32.

23 Fisher and McCluskey, *City of Refuge*, 35.

24 Fisher and McCluskey, 35.

25 Fisher and McCluskey, 35.

26 Fisher and McCluskey, 35.

27 Fisher and McCluskey, 36.

CHAPTER ONE

1 See *ATL: The Untold Story*.

2 See Nelson, "Afro-Futurism."

3 Howard Rambsy writes, "On the level of lyrics, ATLiens contains many raps about street life—a typical approach in hip hop. However, the positioning of the work within sci-fi or outer-space discourse with the liner note booklet resembling a comic book and the alien-related album and song titles empowered OutKast to deviate from the visual narratives about the hood and thug life . . . the juxtaposition of 'ghetto life' with far-off places on OutKast's album reveals a group imagining alternative possibilities for listeners, something beyond the notion of keeping it real" (Rambsy, "Beyond Keeping It Real," 210).

4 OutKast, "D.E.E.P.," *Southernplayalisticadillacmuzik*.

5 OutKast, "ATLiens," *ATLiens*.

6 See Akinyele Umoja's historical study of violence and the resistance in the American South during the civil rights movement titled *We Will Shoot Back*.

7 Nama, *Super Black*, 43.

8 Nama, 43.

9 Gates, *Signifying Monkey*, xxv.

10 OutKast, "Aquemini," *Aquemini*.

11 OutKast, "Da Art of Storytellin' (Part 2)," *Aquemini*.

12 OutKast, "Intro," *Stankonia*.

13 OutKast, "Gasoline Dreams," *Stankonia*.

14 OutKast, "B.O.B.," *Stankonia*.

15 For further discussion of Idlewild, Michigan, see Walker and Wilson, *Black Eden*.

16 Janelle Monáe is featured on the soundtrack but not in the movie.

17 It is important to note Benjamin's discomfort with touring. In a December 2014 interview for *Fader* magazine, Benjamin stated he felt like he sold out as an artist and used his series of black and white jumpsuits to work through his anxiety: "It was a decision. . . . I felt like there was a certain sell-out in a way, because I didn't wanna do it—I knew I was doing it for a reason. So maybe if I'm telling people, 'I am selling out,' then it's not as bad as pretending" (Jaar, "Nicolas Jaar Interviews André 3000").

18 See Bradley, "André Benjamin's Got Something to Say."

19 Royster, *Sounding Like a No-No*, 8.

20 Royster, 11.

CHAPTER TWO

1 For example, see Ernest Gaines's collection of short stories *Bloodline*, Alice Walker's short story "Everyday Use," in the *In Love and Trouble* collection, and Margaret Walker's novel *Jubilee*.

2 See Natasha Trethewey's collection of poetry *Native Guard*, Angie Thomas's novel *The Hate U Give*, and Jesmyn Ward's novel *Sing, Unburied, Sing*. This also extends to the hip-hop coming out of Mississippi, including rappers like David Banner on his 2003 album *Mississippi: The Album* and Big K.R.I.T. on his 2012 debut album *Live from the Underground*.

3 Beatty, *White Boy Shuffle*, 22. SNCC is an acronym for the Student Nonviolent Coordinating Committee. Beatty uses the acronym as a pun in this passage from the novel.

4 Beatty, *White Boy Shuffle*, 22.

5 See Courtney Baker's study, *Humane Insight*.

6 Laymon, *How to Slowly Kill Yourself*, 13.

7 Laymon, 61.

8 See my interview with Brad "Kamikaze" Franklin as part of my *OutKasted Conversations* project, https://www.outkastedconversations.com/outkasted -conversations-brad-kamikaze-franklin-on-southern-hip-hop-and-activism/.

9 Laymon, *How to Slowly Kill Yourself*, 66.

10 Laymon, 61.

11 Wright's autobiography *Black Boy* about growing up Black in Mississippi was first published in 1945.

12 Laymon, *How to Slowly Kill Yourself*, 65.

13 Laymon, 64.

14 Laymon, 70.

15 Laymon, 70.

16 OutKast, "Intro," *Stankonia*.

17 OutKast, "Aquemini," *Aquemini*.

18 Personal interview with Laymon, February 20, 2016.

19 Laymon, *Long Division*, 4.

20 Laymon, 5.

21 Ellison, *Invisible Man*; "King of the Bingo Game," in *Flying Home*.

22 Laymon, 38.

23 Ellison, "King of the Bingo Game," in *Flying Home*, 127.

24 Laymon, *Long Division*, 40.

25 OutKast, "Return of the G," *Aquemini*.

26 OutKast.

27 Carmichael, "The Making of OutKast's *Aquemini*."

28 See Higginbotham, *Righteous Discontent*.

29 Boylorn, *Sweetwater*, 9.

30 Cooper, *Voice from the South*, 9.

31 See Spillers, "Mama's Baby, Papa's Maybe."

32 Hurston, *Their Eyes Were Watching God*.

33 OutKast, "Da Art of Storytellin' (Part 1)," *Aquemini*.

34 Laymon, *Long Division*, 21.

35 Laymon, 245.

36 Laymon, 63.

37 Laymon, 66.

38 Laymon, 247.

39 See Morrison, *Beloved*, 320.

40 Laymon, *Long Division*, 258.

CHAPTER THREE

1 Moten, *In the Break*, 3.

2 Moten, 3.

3 McPherson, *Reconstructing Dixie*, 3.

4 Cox, *Dreaming of Dixie*, 8.

5 Most plantation tours nourish visitors' ideas of a romantic and quaint antebellum South, and avoid the discomfort caused by confronting visitors with the realities of slavery. Yet some tours, such as those to the Whitney Plantation in Edgard, Louisiana, make slavery a central focus. Historical plantation tours remain an extremely popular staple of income for many southern communities, and they lend to the theory that the plantation has multiple uses or "lives." See Jarvis C. McInnis's scholarship on the "afterlives" of plantations, especially "'Behold the Land'"; and Bergner and Nunes, "The Plantation."

6 Robinson, *This Ain't Chicago*, 30.

7 Hartman, "Time of Slavery," 760.

8 The sonic implications of violence against enslaved black people allow us to complicate slavery as an act of violence outside of gendered binaries. For example, see Ashon Crawley's sonic analysis of Harriet Jacobs's *Incidents in the Life of a Slave Girl* in the article "Harriet Jacobs Gets a Hearing."

9 See Mark Anthony Neal's study on contemporary black masculinity titled *Looking for Leroy*. It is also important to note a growing body of scholarship on how *Django Unchained* updates conversations about slavery in popular culture. See "Django Unpacked"; Joi Carr, "Close-Up"; and the collection of essays edited by Oliver C. Speck, *Quentin Tarantino's* Django Unchained.

10 Brown, "The Payback," *The Payback*.

11 Shakur, "Untouchable," *Pac's Life*.

12 The Candieland plantation exists offscreen as well: Evergreen Plantation is in Edgard, Louisiana. Understanding plantations as an industry is important to understanding how plantations in contemporary landscapes influence one's understanding of slavery as a daily experience. See the YouTube miniseries "Ask a Slave," hosted by Azie Mira Dungey, and the blog series "Rebuilding a Slave Cabin," by Carol Jackson and Leoneda Inge, about efforts to rebuild a slave cabin on the grounds of James Madison's Montpelier in Virginia.

13 Sharpe, *Monstrous Intimacies*, 4.

14 Woodward, *Delectable Negro*, 18.

15 Davis, *Southscapes*.

16 Graham and Jones, "An Interview," 427.

17 Tillet, *Sites of Slavery*, 12.

18 Mutter, "'Such a Poor Word,'" 127.

19 Tillet, *Sites of Slavery*, 5.

20 Jones, *Known World*, 15–16.

21 Jones, 137.

22 Jones, 180.

23 Bassard, "Imagining Other Worlds," 413.

24 See Du Bois, "Of the Dawn of Freedom," in *Souls of Black Folk*.

25 Bassard, 408.

26 Jones, *Known World*, 123.

27 Jones, 123.

28 Ikard, "White Supremacy under Fire," 65.

29 Jones, *Known World*, 125.

30 Jones, 124.

31 Jones, 268.

32 Bassard, "Imagining Other Worlds," 417.

33 Donaldson, "Telling Forgotten Stories," 272.

34 Jones, *Known World*, 4.

35 Jones, 13.

36 Jones, 12.

37 Jones, 12.

38 Jones, 13.

39 Jones, 61.

40 Mutter, "'Such a Poor Word,'" 142.

41 Jones, *Known World*, 384.

42 Jones, 386.

43 Donaldson, "Telling Forgotten Stories," 271.

44 Jones, *Known World*, 384.

45 Mutter, "'Such a Poor Word,'" 143.

CHAPTER FOUR

1 See Burton, *Posthuman Rap*; McCarthy, "Notes on Trap"; Lee, "Trap Kings"; and Carmichael, "Culture Wars."

2 See "T.I. x Montreality."

3 The expectation of a short life is also a prominent trope in hip-hop outside of the south; for example, the Notorious B.I.G. and his death-inspired albums *Ready to Die* and *Life after Death*. See Calvente, "'I'm Ready to Die.'"

4 T.I., "Doin' My Job," *Trap Muzik*.

5 T.I., "Act 1: T.I.P.," *T.I. vs. T.I.P.*

6 See Lacan, "The Mirror Stage as Formative of the *I* Function as Revealed in Psychoanalytic Experience," in *Écrits*.

7 T.I., "Act III: T.I. vs. T.I.P.: The Confrontation," *T.I. vs. T.I.P.*

8 Ward, *Where the Line Bleeds*, 2.

9 Ward, 5.

10 Ward, 83.

11 Ward, 126.

12 Ward, 126–127.

13 Ward, *Men We Reaped*, 217.

14 Ward, 219.

15 Ward, 215.

16 Ward, 218.

17 Ward, 231.

BIBLIOGRAPHY

PUBLISHED SOURCES

ATL: The Untold Story of Atlanta's Rise in the Rap Game. Directed by Brad Bernstein, Rick Cikowski, and Brandon Dumlao. New York: VH1, 2014.

Baker, Courtney R. *Humane Insight: Looking at Images of African American Suffering and Death*. Champaign: University of Illinois Press, 2015.

Bassard, Katherine Clay. "Imagining Other Worlds: Race, Gender, and the 'Power Line' in Edward P. Jones's *The Known World*." *African American Review* 42, no. 3 (2008): 407–419.

Beatty, Paul. *The White Boy Shuffle: A Novel*. New York: Picador, 1996.

Bergner, Gwen, and Zita Cristina Nunes, eds. "The Plantation, the Postplantation, and the Afterlives of Slavery." Special issue. *American Literature* 91, no. 3 (September 2019): 447–689.

The Black Godfather. Directed by Reginald Hudlin. Los Gatos, CA: Netflix, 2019.

Boylorn, Robin. *Sweetwater: Black Women and Narratives of Resilience*. New York: Peter Lang, 2012.

Bradley, Regina. "André Benjamin's Got Something to Say: The Evolution of OutKast's Style Maven." *Red Bull Music Academy*, February 12, 2019. https://daily.redbullmusicacademy.com/2019/02/the-evolution-of-andre-3000-style.

———. "The Mountaintop Ain't Flat." *Savannah TEDx*, May 2019. http://www.tedxsavannah.com/talks/the-mountaintop-aint-flat/.

Burton, Justin Adams. *Posthuman Rap*. New York: Oxford University Press, 2017.

Calvente, Lisa B. Y. "'I'm Ready to Die': The Notorious B.I.G., Black Love, and Death." In *The Oxford Handbook of Hip Hop Music*, edited by Justin D. Burton and Jason Lee Oakes. 2018. https://doi.org/10.1093/oxfordhb/9780190281090.013.9.

Carmichael, Rodney. "Culture Wars: Trap Music Keeps Atlanta on Hip-Hop's Cutting Edge. Why Can't the City Embrace It?" *NPR Music*, March 15, 2017. https://www.npr.org/sections/therecord/2017/03/15/520133445/culture-wars-trap-innovation-atlanta-hip-hop.

———. "The Making of OutKast's *Aquemini*." *Creative Loafing*, June 24, 2010. https://creativeloafing.com/content-168326-the-making-of-outkast-s-aquemini.

Carr, Joi, ed. "Close-Up: *Django Unchained*." *Black Camera* 7, no. 2 (Spring 2016): 37–93.

Cooper, Anna Julia. *A Voice from the South* (Dover Thrift Editions). Mineola, NY: Dover, 2016.

Cox, Karen L. *Destination Dixie: Tourism and Southern History*. Gainesville: University Press of Florida, 2014.

———. *Dreaming of Dixie: How the South was Created in American Popular Culture*. Chapel Hill: University of North Carolina Press, 2011.

Crawley, Ashon. "Harriet Jacobs Gets a Hearing." *Current Musicology* 93 (Spring 2012): 33–55.

Davis, Thadious. *Southscapes: Geographies of Race, Region, and Literature*. Chapel Hill: University of North Carolina Press, 2011.

"The Dirty South." *Hip Hop Evolution*. Directed by Darby Wheeler. Toronto: Banger Films, 2019.

Django Unchained. Directed by Quentin Tarantino. Culver City, CA: Columbia Pictures, 2012.

"Django Unpacked." *Transition* magazine, no. 112 (2013): 1–172.

Donaldson, Susan V. "Telling Forgotten Stories of Slavery in the Postmodern South." *Southern Literary Journal* 40, no. 2 (2008): 267–283.

Du Bois, W. E. B. *The Souls of Black Folk* (Dover Thrift Editions). Mineola, NY: Dover, 1994.

Dungey, Azie Mira. "Ask a Slave: The Web Series." *YouTube*, 2013. https://www.youtube.com/channel/UCHPZR1lUMS47BA-N2Ihrtlg.

Ellison, Ralph. *Flying Home and Other Stories*. New York: Vintage, 1998.

———. *Invisible Man*. New York: Vintage, 1995.

"Faith Is What You Make It." Produced by WABE/PRX. *Bottom of the Map*. September 9, 2019. https://podcasts.apple.com/us/podcast/faith-is-what-you-make-it/id1462206435?i=1000449070680.

Faniel, Maco. *Hip Hop in Houston: The Origin and the Legacy*. Charleston: History Press, 2013.

Fisher, Rudolph and John McCluskey, eds. *The City of Refuge [New and Expanded Edition]: The Collected Stories of Rudolph Fisher*. Columbia: University of Missouri Press, 2018.

Formwalt, Lee. *Looking Back, Moving Forward: The Southwest Georgia Freedom Struggle, 1814–2014*. Albany, GA: Albany Civil Rights Institute, 2014.

Gaines, Ernest. *Bloodline: Five Stories* (1st Contemporaries Edition). New York: Vintage, 1997.

Gates, Henry Louis. *The Signifying Monkey: A Theory of African American Literary Criticism*. Oxford: Oxford University Press, 1988.

George, Nelson. *Post-Soul Nation: The Explosive, Contradictory, Triumphant, and Tragic 1980s as Experienced by African Americans (Previously Known as Blacks and Before That Negroes)*. New York: Penguin Random House, 2004.

Graham, Maryemma, and Edward P. Jones. "An Interview with Edward P. Jones." *African American Review* (2008): 421–438.

Grem, Darren. "'The South Got Something to Say': Atlanta's Dirty South and the Southernization of Hip-Hop America." *Southern Cultures* 12, no. 4 (2006): 55–73.

Hartman, Saidiya. "The Time of Slavery." *South Atlantic Quarterly* 101, no. 4 (2002): 757–777.

Higginbotham, Evelyn Brooks. *Righteous Discontent: The Women's Movement in the Black Baptist Church, 1880–1920*. Cambridge: Harvard University Press, 1994.

Hobson, Maurice J. *The Legend of the Black Mecca: Politics and Class in the Making of Modern Atlanta*. Chapel Hill: University of North Carolina Press, 2017.

Hurston, Zora Neale. *Their Eyes Were Watching God*. 1937. Reprint, New York: Amistad, 2006.

Ikard, David. "White Supremacy under Fire: The Unrewarded Perspective in Edward P. Jones's *The Known World*." *MELUS* 36, no. 3 (Fall 2011): 63–85.

Jaar, Nicolas. "Nicolas Jaar Interviews André 3000." *Fader* magazine, December 3, 2014. https://www.thefader.com/2014/12/03/andre-3000-art-show-jumpsuits-nicolas-jaar-interview.

Jackson, Carol, and Leoneda Inge. "Rebuilding a Slave Cabin: 'Proud of the Work We've Done.'" *WUNC*, February 18, 2014. https://www.wunc.org/post/rebuilding-slave-cabin-proud-work-we-ve-done.

Jones, Edward P. *The Known World*. New York: Harper, 2003.

King, Martin Luther, Jr. *Why We Can't Wait*. New York: Signet Classics, 2000.

Lacan, Jacques. *Écrits: The First Complete Edition in English*. Translated by Bruce Fink. New York: W. W. Norton and Company, 2005.

Laymon, Kiese. *How to Slowly Kill Yourself and Others in America*. Chicago: Agate, 2013.

———. *Long Division*. Chicago: Agate, 2013.

Lee, Christina. "Trap Kings: How the Hip-Hop Sub-Genre Dominated the Decade." *Guardian*, August 13, 2015. https://www.theguardian.com/music/2015/aug/13/trap-kings-how-hip-hop-sub-genre-dominated-decade.

McCarthy, Jesse. "Notes on Trap." *N+1* magazine, no. 32 (Fall 2018). https://nplusonemag.com/issue-32/essays/notes-on-trap/.

McInnis, Jarvis C. "'Behold the Land': W. E. B. Du Bois, Cotton Futures, and the Afterlife of the Plantation in the U.S. South." *Global South* 10, no. 2 (2016): 70–98.

McIntyre, Rebecca Cawood. *Souvenirs of the Old South: Northern Tourism and Southern Mythology*. Gainesville: University Press of Florida, 2011.

McPherson, Tara. *Reconstructing Dixie: Race, Gender, and Nostalgia in the Imagined South*. Durham: Duke University Press, 2003.

Morrison, Toni. *Beloved*. New York: Vintage, 2004.

Moten, Fred. *In the Break: The Aesthetics of the Black Radical Tradition*. Minneapolis: University of Minnesota Press, 2003.

Mutter, Sarah Mahurin. "'Such a Poor Word for a Wondrous Thing': Thingness and Recovery of the Human in *The Known World*." *Southern Literary Journal* 43, no. 2 (Spring 2011): 125–146.

Nama, Adilifu. *Super Black: American Pop Culture and Black Superheroes*. Austin: University of Texas Press, 2011.

Neal, Mark Anthony. *Looking for Leroy: Illegible Black Masculinities*. New York: New York University Press, 2013.

———. *Soul Babies: Black Popular Culture and the Post-Soul Aesthetic*. New York: Routledge, 2001.

Neff, Ali Colleen. *Let the World Listen Right: The Mississippi Delta Hip-Hop Story*. Jackson: University of Mississippi Press, 2009.

Nelson, Alondra. "Afro-Futurism: Past Future Visions." *Color Lines* 3, no. 1 (2000): 34–47.

Perry, Imani. *Prophets of the Hood: Politics and Poetics in Hip Hop*. Durham, NC: Duke University Press, 2004.

Rambsy, Howard. "Beyond Keeping It Real: OutKast, the Funk Connection, and Afrofuturism." *American Studies* 52, no. 4 (2013): 205–216.

Robinson, Zandria F. *This Ain't Chicago: Race, Class, and Regional Identity in the Post-Soul South*. Chapel Hill: University of North Carolina Press, 2014.

Royster, Francesca. *Sounding Like a No-No: Queer Sounds and Eccentric Acts in the Post-Soul Era*. Ann Arbor: University of Michigan Press, 2012.

Sharpe, Christina. *Monstrous Intimacies: Making Post-Slavery Subjects*. Durham, NC: Duke University Press, 2010.

Speck, Oliver C., ed. *Quentin Tarantino's* Django Unchained: *The Continuation of Metacinema*. New York: Bloomsbury, 2014.

Spillers, Hortense. "Mama's Baby, Papa's Maybe: An American Grammar Book," *Diacritics* 17, no. 2 (Summer 1987): 64–81.

Thomas, Angie. *The Hate U Give*. New York: HarperCollins, 2017.

Tillet, Salamishah. *Sites of Slavery: Citizenship and Racial Democracy in the Post-Civil Rights Imagination*. Durham, NC: Duke University Press, 2012.

"T.I. x Montreality: Interview," *YouTube*, August 2, 2017. https://www.youtube.com/watch?v=Gn_IryVKdmE.

Trethewey, Natasha. *Native Guard: Poems*. Boston: Houghton Mifflin, 2007.

Umoja, Akinyele. *We Will Shoot Back: Armed Resistance in the Mississippi Freedom Movement*. New York: New York University Press, 2013.

Walker, Alice. *In Love and Trouble: Stories of Black Women*. 1973. Reprint, Boston: Mariner Books, 2003.

Walker, Lewis, and Benjamin C. Wilson. *Black Eden: The Idlewild Community*. East Lansing: Michigan State University Press, 2007.

Walker, Margaret. *Jubilee* (Anniversary Edition). Boston: Mariner Books, 2016.

Ward, Jesmyn. *Men We Reaped*. New York: Bloomsbury, 2013.

———. *Salvage the Bones: A Novel*. New York: Bloomsbury, 2011.

———. *Sing, Unburied, Sing: A Novel*. New York: Scribner, 2017.

———. *Where the Line Bleeds*. Chicago: Agate, 2008.

Woodward, Vincent. *The Delectable Negro: Human Consumption and Homoeroticism within US Culture*. New York: New York University Press, 2014.

Wright, Richard. *Black Boy* (75th Anniversary Edition). New York: Harper, 2020.

DISCOGRAPHY

Banner, David. *Mississippi: The Album*. Universal Records, 2003.

Big K.R.I.T. *Live from the Underground*. Cinematic Music Group/Def Jam Recordings, 2012.

Brown, James. *The Payback*. Polydor, 1973.

OutKast. *Aquemini*. LaFace Records, 1998.

———. *ATLiens*. LaFace Records, 1996.

———. *Southernplayalisticadillacmuzik*. LaFace Records, 1994.

———. *Speakerboxxx/The Love Below*. LaFace Records, 2003.

———. *Stankonia*. LaFace Records, 2000.

Shakur, Tupac. *Pac's Life*. Amaru Entertainment, 2006.

T.I. *I'm Serious*. Arista Records, 2001.

———. *T.I. vs. T.I.P.* Atlantic Records, 2007.

———. *Trap Muzik*. Atlantic Records, 2003.

———. *Urban Legend*. Atlantic Records, 2004.

INDEX